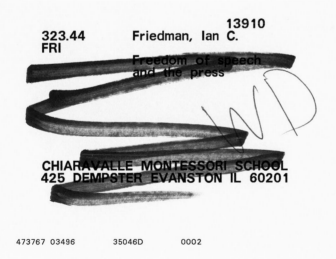

FREEDOM OF SPEECH AND THE PRESS

AMERICAN RIGHTS

FREEDOM OF SPEECH AND THE PRESS

IAN C. FRIEDMAN

Facts On File, Inc.

Freedom of Speech and the Press

Facts On File, Inc.
132 West 31st Street
New York NY 10001

Library of Congress Cataloging-in-Publication Data
Friedman, Ian C.
   Freedom of speech and the press / Ian C. Friedman.
      p. cm. — (American rights)
   Includes bibliographical references and index.
   ISBN 0-8160-5662-5
   1. Freedom of speech—United States—History—Juvenile literature. 2. Freedom of the press—United States—History—Juvenile literature. I. Title. II. Series.
   JC591.F843 2005
   323.44'3'0973—dc222004021003

Facts On File books are available at special discounts when purchased in bulk quantities for businesses, associations, institutions, or sales promotions. Please call our Special Sales Department in New York at (212) 967-8800 or (800) 322-8755.

You can find Facts On File on the World Wide Web at http://www.factsonfile.com

Text design by Erika K. Arroyo
Cover design by Pehrsson Design
Maps and graphs by Sholto Ainslie

Printed in the United States of America

VB FOF 10 9 8 7 6 5 4 3 2

This book is printed on acid-free paper.

For my parents
Marcia and Leon Friedman

Note on Photos

Many of the illustrations and photographs used in this book are old, historical images. The quality of the prints is not always up to modern standards because in many cases the originals are from glass negatives or the originals are damaged. The content of the illustrations, however, made their inclusion important despite problems in reproduction.

Contents

Acknowledgments

Thanks to my editor at Facts On File, Nicole Bowen, and to Laura Shauger for their assistance.

I am also grateful to the people, both famous and anonymous, who created the invaluable rights to free speech and free press in the United States and to those who have served and sacrificed so that others may enjoy these rights.

My greatest thanks go to my family. To my wife, Darlene, for her love and support and to my children who provided me with unique and cherished diversions during the time I was writing this book: Evan with delightful stories of his day, Mason with his quick visits for a smile and hug, and Lily with her wonderful arrival to my life.

Introduction

In 1860, Frederick Douglass, a prominent abolitionist speaker and writer and a former slave, addressed an audience in Boston a week after a mob in that city had disrupted a meeting held to discuss ways to end slavery in the South. With eloquent passion he stated: "Liberty is meaningless where the right to utter one's thoughts and opinions has ceased to exist. That, of all rights, is the dread of tyrants. It is the right which they first of all strike down. They know its power."

His words inspired those assembled and informed the countless number of people who would soon read them in newspapers. They represent the simple yet radical belief in the value of free expression, specifically the rights to freedom of speech and the press that has made the Constitution of the United States and American society a shining light for those seeking liberty for well over 200 years.

The American rights to free speech and free press are detailed in the U.S. Constitution's First Amendment: "Congress shall make no law . . . abridging the freedom of speech, or of the press . . ." But these words are not as simple as they appear. How they have been understood and applied have been at the center of many of the fiercest debates in American history, and arguments over what exactly is meant by "free speech" and "free press" remain as common as ever today.

U.S. history has been shaped and reflected in these conflicts over the freedoms of speech and the press. The Constitution itself and the First Amendment rights that provide it with so much power were created because of a desire among the founders to

This portrait shows Frederick Douglass, whose written and spoken words helped end slavery in the United States. *(Library of Congress, Prints and Photographs Division [LC-USZ62-15887])*

ensure that Americans had protections from government interference into their individual expression.

Throughout the 19th century, the rights to free speech and free press accompanied the most important and complex issues of the time. These rights were asserted when political bickering threatened free expression, and they were the most powerful weapons in the abolitionists' long and successful battle to end slavery. The freedoms of speech and the press were tested by the Civil War and found new power and controversy with the growing influence of immigrants and labor unions.

As newspaper circulation skyrocketed as the country entered the 20th century, the rights to a free press were both blamed for irresponsible news reporting and credited with leading social reform. Before and after World War I, free speech advocates faced their stiffest opposition from those who feared that criticism of the United States was equal to betrayal of the United States.

The growing number of free expression controversies and the complex nature of many of these quarrels then led to the growing importance in American society of the U.S. Supreme Court, which would take the lead in defining the limits of these freedoms in order to prevent the dangers that could come from saying or printing anything, without regard to individual and national security.

During the second half of the 20th century, freedom of speech and of the press played an even more critical role than ever before in U.S. history and culture. This period was marked by clashes over national loyalty and patriotism during the McCarthyism era; the racial division and unity of the Civil Rights movement; the obscenity battles in magazines, movies, television, and radio; the Vietnam War; the political scandal of Watergate; and the technological innovation of the Internet. Each of these events was powerfully influenced by the rights to free speech and free press. These episodes also had an enormous impact on shifting the views Americans had on the freedoms of speech and the press, views that continue to evolve.

The American debate over the rights to free speech and free press has been constant and intense because, as Frederick Douglass pointed out, these rights possess tremendous power. They are powers that have endured more than 200 years of battle and emerged tougher, wiser, and more inclusive. As they have throughout American history, the rights to freedom of speech and freedom of the press stand ready to take their place at the center of the most important issues facing the United States.

Foundations of Free Speech and Press

FREE SPEECH AND PRESS IN THE ANCIENT WORLD AND MIDDLE AGES

Americans' rights of freedom of speech and the press trace their roots to societies that existed long before the creation of the United States. One of the earliest examples of the struggle for these liberties comes from ancient Greece. In the city-state of Athens around 440 B.C., free men enjoyed rights of free speech unknown to earlier generations. A few decades later, however, the clash between the desire for free speech and the concern for the effect it had on society—a theme that has continued throughout history—occurred when the Athenian philosopher Socrates upset many with his teaching style and religious views. Socrates' belief that "the unexamined life is not worth living" reflected a frequent and sometimes critical view of Athenian society.

In 399 B.C., Socrates was put on trial for corrupting the youth and insulting the gods. He was given a choice to leave Athens and live in exile or die by drinking a cup of poisonous hemlock. Explaining that "I was really too honest a man to be a politician and live," Socrates chose to be executed, making him a martyr (a person who suffers or dies for the sake of a principle) for the right to free expression.

Ancient Rome also provides examples of people suffering for their speech. Although there was no official state censorship in ancient Rome, people were often forced to leave, put in jail, or killed for criticizing the government too vocally.

One notable supporter of free speech in ancient Rome was Marcus Porcius Cato, who was better known as Cato the Younger. His opposition to Roman emperor Julius Caesar led to his exile and suicide, but his reputation as an honest statesman has made him a respected symbol of free speech for centuries.

The next significant event in the development of freedom of speech and the press occurred in England in 1215. It was then that a group of English noblemen, upset about heavy taxes and other abuses forced by King John, threatened revolt. Hoping to avoid conflict, the king agreed to sign the Magna Carta (which means "great charter" in Latin). The Magna Carta guaranteed certain rights to English noblemen, including trial by jury. The Magna Carta did not provide rights for freedom of speech and the press, and the liberties it provided seem weak by current standards in the United States. But it did establish an end to absolute power of English monarchs. Its ideals, such as a belief that a legitimate and fair

This engraving depicts the Greek philosopher Socrates, whose choice of death over exile as punishment for criticizing Greek society made him a hero to supporters of free speech. *(Library of Congress, Prints and Photographs Division [LC-USZ61-1503])*

government requires the support of the people, later became key parts of the Declaration of Independence and the U.S. Constitution, which helped form the foundation for American freedom of speech and the press.

GUTENBERG'S PRINTING PRESS

In 1459, one event revolutionized not only the history of freedom of speech and the press but also changed the history of the world: the invention of the printing press by Johann Gutenberg of Germany. Gutenberg's printing press used a process of movable type that made the creation of many copies of a manuscript far easier and faster than ever before. At first, this

Inventor Johann Gutenberg is depicted in this painting alongside his printing press. *(Library of Congress, Prints and Photographs Division [LC-USZ62-101612])*

invention was used mainly to make bibles and other religious literature available to the general population. But soon people like William Caxton, who set up England's first printing press in 1476, began reproducing books of all kinds, including translations of foreign literature.

CENSORSHIP IN GREAT BRITAIN

By the early 16th century, this new method of printing led to the spread of ideas that occasionally criticized government and religious leaders. Very quickly, the Catholic Church required all printers to have licenses and prohibited the printing of anything without the approval of church authorities. Many other government officials throughout Europe who were not associated with the Catholic Church did the same thing, including the English king Henry VIII, who ruled that all published work had to be approved by an official *censor* (a person with authority to examine and forbid the publication of documents).

Those who wrote opinions considered critical that somehow did get published were often punished severely. One example is John Stubbs. In 1579, Stubbs wrote a book critical of England's Queen Elizabeth's upcoming marriage. When the queen learned of this, her agents ordered all copies of the book burned and the right hand of the author chopped off with a mallet.

Another tragic victim of free press restriction was English printer John Twyn. In 1663, Twyn was found guilty of treason for publishing a book that expressed the belief that the king was accountable to the people. Told by the prison chaplain that he might be spared his life if he disclosed the book's author, Twyn refused, saying "Better one suffer than many." He was then executed. Twyn has since become an honored symbol of the press's freedom of protecting the identity of sources.

During the late 16th and early 17th centuries in England, the strongest weapon of press restriction was the Star Chamber. The Star Chamber was a small group of advisers handpicked by the king that met in private and dealt with state security. At first, it was created to bring powerful people to trial but eventually it became a court attacking the king's enemies.

Despite the power of the Star Chamber and the intimidating punishments it enforced, people continued to run secret printing presses that occasionally distributed material full of ideas and opinions considered seditious *libel* (language inciting people to rebel against state authority). In 1641, largely because of the brave persistence of these printers, the English Parliament disbanded the Star Chamber.

Although the Star Chamber was abolished, English authorities were not eager to expand rights to free speech and press. Reliance on a licensing system for printers continued even though growing numbers of people opposed it. The most powerful expression of opposition to licensing requirements before books or pamphlets could be published was offered by the great English poet and essayist John Milton.

In his speech *Areopagitica* (named after the market area in ancient Greece where ideas were traditionally exchanged), Milton argued against *prior restraint* (prohibiting distribution of expression before publication) with reasoning that is still used by supporters of free speech and press more than 350 years later. Among Milton's views was the belief that in trying to protect people from lies, censorship actually kept people from learning the truth. He also ques-

"Let truth and falsehood grapple; who ever knew truth put to the worse, in a free and open encounter?"

—*John Milton,*
Areopagitica, *1644*

tioned the ability to select fair and honest censors, stating "How shall the licensors themselves be confided in, unless we can confer upon them, or they assume to themselves, above all others in the land, the grace of infallibility and uncorruptedness?" Finally, he described the danger of censoring books, saying ". . . he who

European Influence on American Rights to Free Speech and Press, 399 B.C.–1644

1. **399 B.C., Ancient Greece:** Leading philosopher Socrates chooses suicide over exile after being convicted of criticizing Athenian society.
2. **509–270 B.C., Ancient Rome:** People are often jailed, exiled, or executed for criticism of the government.
3. **1459, Mainz, Germany:** Johann Gutenberg invents movable type printing press.
4. **1644, London, England:** Poet John Milton forcefully argues against governmental controls over free speech and press.

North Sea

ATLANTIC

OCEAN

Black Sea

Mediterranean Sea

N

Note: Map shown with modern boundaries for reference.

| 0 | | 500 miles |
| 0 | | 500 km |

destroys a good book kills reason . . . A good book is the precious lifeblood of a master spirit, embalmed and treasured up on purpose to a life beyond life."

Milton's words had little immediate impact; it would be 50 years until the licensing requirements were dropped in England. Even when the licensing laws were abolished, it did not lead to the kind of freedom of speech and the press that exists today. Instead, it delayed the punishment given to those who said or wrote things that the government (and in some cases the church) did not approve of. Until the late 18th century in England, the law of seditious libel made it a crime to print or say anything intended to damage the king or government. Violators were routinely fined, imprisoned, or even tortured for what in the United States today is considered ordinary political debate. Criticism considered harmful to someone's reputation was also punished whether it was *slander* (false accusations) or true.

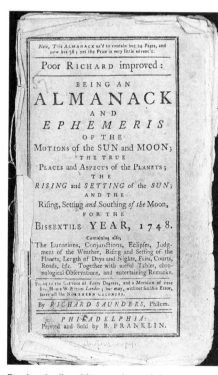

Benjamin Franklin, author of the enormously popular *Poor Richard's Almanack*, was an early advocate of freedom of the press. *(Library of Congress, Prints and Photographs Division [LC-USZ62-75475])*

FREE EXPRESSION IN THE AMERICAN COLONIES

In the British colonies in America, across the Atlantic Ocean from England, the words of Milton and the tradition of free speech and press found a welcome home, despite the often tight restrictions on free expression enforced by colonial governments.

The first public book burning took place in 1650 in Boston because authorities there believed that the religious ideas contained in William Pynchon's *The Meritorious Price of Our Redemption* conflicted with Massachusetts's long-established religion. In 1690, the colonies' first newspaper, *Publick Occurrences Both Foreign and Domestic,* was printed in Boston but was shut down after only one issue, mainly because government leaders disapproved of its content.

An important milestone for free expression in the colonies took place in 1721 when the publisher of the *New England Courant,* James Franklin, was jailed for criticism of the British government printed in his newspaper. While Franklin remained in jail, his

BENJAMIN FRANKLIN
Early American Press Hero

In the early 1720s, more than a half-century before America's split from Great Britain, 16-year-old Benjamin Franklin expressed his opposition to the political leadership in his native Boston through a fictional character named Mrs. Silence Dogood, whose views were anonymously published in Franklin's brother's independent newspaper. As Mrs. Dogood, Franklin asserted "I am a mortal enemy to arbitrary government and unlimited power."

By age 22, Franklin opened his own printing office in Philadelphia, where he published *The Pennsylvania Gazette* and his annual *Poor Richard's Almanack*. He helped popularize many new publishing ideas, including illustrated news stories, letters to the editor, and even cartoons. He was a firm believer in the power of the press to help everyone understand the news, including people who had not learned to read.

younger brother, 16-year-old Benjamin Franklin, continued to publish the paper.

Benjamin Franklin, who would later become one of the most important leaders of America's revolutionary movement, struck an early blow for liberty of expression by publishing the essays of John Trenchard and Thomas Gordon, who wrote under the *pseudonym* (fake name) of Cato. They took this name in honor of the Roman statesman who is considered a pioneer in free speech. Their essays, known as *Cato's Letters,* were enormously popular and influential in the American colonies. *Cato's Letters,* written between 1720–23, concerned the colonies' relationship with England and the principles that should guide fair and legitimate governments.

One of the most widely quoted of *Cato's Letters* was #15, entitled "Of Freedom of Speech." In this essay, the authors explain that all liberties depend upon the freedom of speech:

> *Without freedom of thought, there can be no such thing as wisdom; and no such thing as publick liberty, without freedom of speech: Which is the right of every man, as far as by it he does not hurt and control the right of another; and this is the only check which it ought to suffer, the only bounds which it ought to know. This sacred privilege is so essential to free government, that the security of property;*

> "Whoever would overthrow the liberty of the nation, must begin by subduing the freedom of speech."
>
> —*John Trenchard and Thomas Gordon,* Cato's Letters #15, *1720*

and the freedom of speech, always go together; and in those wretched countries where a man can not call his tongue his own, he can scarce call any thing else his own.

Censorship of speech was also tightly enforced in the American colonies. The Virginia Code of 1610 included the death penalty for speaking against Christianity or the governor. During the early 17th century, thousands of people were brought before various colonial assemblies and punished or tortured for even mild criticism of public officials. Proof that criticism was true was no protection. In fact, truthful criticism was usually viewed as worse than slander because of its ability to effectively undermine authority.

THE TRIAL OF JOHN PETER ZENGER

A critical milestone in the history of American free expression, particularly freedom of the press, occurred with the trial of John Peter Zenger in 1735. Zenger was the publisher of the *New York Weekly Journal,* a newspaper that had included criticism of New York's colonial governor William Cosby. The criticism ranged from accusations of incompetence in defending the colony against the French to tampering with jury trials and elections.

Zenger was arrested and jailed by authority of the governor on charges of "raising sedition." The *New York Weekly Journal* missed printing only one issue, then reappeared with a note from the defiant Zenger that the paper would continue to be edited "thro the hole of the door in the prison." Zenger's wife and friends actually kept the paper running during the nine months he was in jail.

The trial of John Peter Zenger attracted a lot of attention and news of it entertained the people of New York while frustrating the governor. Zenger was defended by one of the most famous lawyers in colonial America, Andrew Hamilton. The nearly 80-year-old Hamilton refused to accept a fee from Zenger because he considered the case crucial to the future of liberty.

During the trial, the prosecutor explained the traditional British rule of seditious libel, pointing out that proof that Zenger published criticism of the governor, regardless of its truth, was all that was needed for a conviction. In addition, he noted that if the criticism was true, it would actually be a more severe crime because that could lead people to distrust the government and commit more crimes of sedition.

The 1735 trial of John Peter Zenger established the concept that published truth could not be considered libel. *(Library of Congress, Prints and Photographs Division [LC-USZ62-48739])*

Hamilton responded to these arguments by stunning the court with the admission that Zenger had printed the criticisms complained about by the prosecution. "I cannot think it proper," said Hamilton, "to deny the publication of a complaint which I think is the right of every free born subject to make." He went on to assert, "The words themselves must be libelous—that is false, scandalous, and seditious or else we are not guilty."

Dressed in his traditional brilliant red robe and giant wig, Chief Justice James DeLancey then sharply told Hamilton, "You cannot be admitted . . . to give the truth of libel in evidence." Quietly ignoring the judge, Hamilton turned to the jury and stated, "Then, gentlemen of the jury, it is to you we must now appeal as witnesses to the truth of the facts we have offered and are denied the liberty to prove . . . You are citizens of New York [and the facts] are notoriously known to be true; and therefore in your justice lies our safety."

Hamilton explained that the jury should be allowed to consider the truth of the criticism in determining Zenger's innocence,

> "The trial of Zenger in 1735 was the morning star of that liberty which . . . revolutionized America."
>
> —*Gouverneur Morris (1752–1816), author of Preamble to the Constitution*

REMEMBERING JOHN PETER ZENGER

The jury assumed the powers that Hamilton had boldly claimed it had and found Zenger not guilty. Chief Justice DeLancey could have set aside the verdict but decided not to in order to avoid a popular uprising. Because a jury verdict could not change the law, the Zenger decision did not strike down the law of seditious libel. But it was enormously influential because it demonstrated that colonial America did not have to follow British customs, that government authority could be criticized, and perhaps most important, that truth was a defense against charges of libel. This not guilty verdict represents a key event in the development of the American concept of liberty because it shows that freedom of thought and speech is an inborn right not to be denied by government authority.

John Peter Zenger was born in Germany in 1697 and came to New York at age 13. He worked as an indentured servant for a printer until opening his own printing press. Zenger died in 1746 at age 49. The *New York Weekly Journal,* which had been the center of so much controversy just a decade earlier, continued publishing under the direction of his wife and later his son until 1751, when the life of this newspaper came to an end.

Despite his enormous impact on the American tradition of freedom of the press, Zenger's legacy is often ignored; only one school in the United States, an elementary school in New York City, honors his name.

reasoning that it is fair for people to complain about "men who injure and oppress the people under their administration; provoke them to cry out . . . and complain; and then make that very complaint the foundation for new oppressions and prosecutions."

Following the trial, an English newspaper printed an account of it, noting that its outcome had "made a great noise in the world." That noise would become much louder with the growing struggle for independence in the American colonies and the evolution of a new nation, the United States of America, built largely on a foundation of the freedoms of speech and the press.

2

Defining Free Speech and Press in a New Nation

In the years immediately following the Zenger decision, colonial newspapers enjoyed broader freedoms. Cases of seditious libel were rare and even when they did occur, they did not result in one successful prosecution of the accused. Yet most of the press in the American colonies during this time did not strongly attack British authority, even though the regulations placed on Americans were relatively light. That changed in 1765 when the British Parliament passed the Stamp Act.

THE PATH TO THE AMERICAN REVOLUTION

The Stamp Act required that publishers pay a special tax in order to produce all books, newspapers, and official documents. This tax was difficult for American publishers to bear. Many were struggling even before this extra financial burden was enforced. Across the colonies, many publishers shut down, but others reacted with sharp assertions of liberty that would later come to mark the reasoning for revolution.

The British imposed the Stamp Tax largely to raise money needed to run the colonies following the costly, though victorious years of battle in the French and Indian wars. Many Americans were offended that they would be forced to pay such a tax when they did not have representation in the British Parliament. The outcry of "No taxation without representation!" was powerful enough that the British repealed the tax within a year of its passage.

However, the entire Stamp Act episode set the stage for the tense period that followed in which patriotic beliefs of liberty and independence were aroused. In fact, the years leading to the American Revolution are rich with spoken and written words reflecting the colonists' desire for freedom of speech and press, as reflected by the volume and intensity of American opposition to new British taxes. Conflict between the mother country, Great Britain, and the rebellious offspring in the American colonies became war on June 1, 1775, in Massachusetts at the battle of Lexington. Soon, perhaps the most eloquent words spoken during the war were stated by Virginia Patriot Patrick Henry:

The war is actually begun! The next gale that sweeps from the north will bring to our ears the clash of resounding arms! Our brethren are already in the field! Why stand we here idle? What is it that gentlemen wish? What would they have? Is life so dear, or peace so sweet, as to be purchased at the price of chains and slavery? Forbid it, Almighty God! I know not what course others may take; but as for me, give me liberty or give me death!

THOMAS PAINE'S *COMMON SENSE*

In addition to the powerful words of leaders such as Patrick Henry, the movement for American independence gained even more momentum from pioneers of the free press. Among the most prominent of these writers was Thomas Paine, an Englishman who arrived in the American colonies in 1774.

In January 1776, Paine published his fiery pro-independence pamphlet *Common Sense*. In it he radically attacked the institution of *monarchies* (governments run by kings and queens) by arguing that these kinds of governments are corrupt and unaccountable to the people. Paine also analyzed the colonies' relationship with Great Britain and strongly rebutted common arguments against revolution:

Thomas Paine, the author of *Common Sense*, wrote some of the most memorable and influential words of the American Revolution. *(Library of Congress, Prints and Photographs Division [LC-USZ62-5243])*

*I have heard it asserted by some, that as America hath flourished
under her former connection with Great Britain, that the same connection is necessary towards her future happiness, and will always
have the same effect. Nothing can be more fallacious than this kind
of argument. We may as well assert, that because a child has
thrived upon milk, that it is never to have meat . . . America would
have flourished as much, and probably much more, had no European power had any thing to do with her. The commerce by which
she hath enriched herself are the necessaries of life, and will always
have a market while eating is the custom of Europe.*

In *Common Sense,* Paine also offered a description of the form of
government he believed should take the place of British rule, providing a blueprint for what would later become the legislative and
executive branches of U.S. government. Although Paine did not
specifically address the issues of freedom of speech and the press, his
views represented exactly the kind of political expression that the
founders of the United States would seek to protect. The influence
of *Common Sense* was enormous. Within three months of its publication, more than 100,000 copies had been sold in the colonies, the
population of which was less than 4 million at that time.

DECLARING INDEPENDENCE

Less than a year after the publication of *Common Sense,* the Virginia
Declaration of Rights was written. Authored by Continental Congress delegate George Mason, this document served as a model for
the various state constitutions that were springing up after the
beginning of the American Revolution.

The Virginia Declaration of Rights also had a profound influence on the composition of the Declaration of Independence, the
U.S. Constitution, and the Bill of Rights, which would soon follow.
It also placed freedom of expression, particularly freedom of the
press, at the forefront of valued rights in a way that had never been
done before. Article XII of the Virginia Declaration of Rights states:
"That the freedom of the press is one of the greatest bulwarks of
liberty and can never be restrained but by despotic governments."

Many other state constitutions reflected the emphasis on freedom of the press that Mason had included in the Virginia Declaration of Rights. In 1788, John Adams included in a draft of the
Massachusetts Declaration of Rights that "the liberty of the press is

This painting, showing the signing of the Declaration of Independence, hangs in the U.S. Capitol. *(Library of Congress, Prints and Photographs Division [LC-H8-C01-063-A])*

essential to the security of freedom in a state; it ought not, therefore, to be restrained in this commonwealth."

The drive for freedom of speech and the press continued with the July 4, 1776, signing of the Declaration of Independence. Although this document gave birth to a new nation, the United States of America, many Americans were content to simply have their own country, separate from Great Britain but very similar in the rights of citizens.

For others, such as Thomas Jefferson and James Madison, however, that was not enough. They believed that the creation of this new nation provided an opportunity to expand previously understood notions of rights and liberty. Unlike in Great Britain, where it was still against the law for people to criticize the government, the Declaration of Independence asserted that in the United States there were rights that government should not control: "We hold these truths to be self-evident, that all men are created equal, that they are endowed by their creator with certain unalienable rights, that among these are life, liberty and the pursuit of happiness—that to secure these rights, governments are instituted among men, deriving their just powers from the consent of the governed. . . ."

These powerful words explained radical ideas for the protection of liberty. Among the most radical ideas were that governments were created by and for the people and certain freedoms, such as those of speech and the press, could not be granted or denied by governments. Rather, governments existed to protect these rights for the people.

THE CONSTITUTION AND BILL OF RIGHTS

Eleven years after the Declaration of Independence detailed the ideals on which the government of the United States would be built, the Constitution established how the government would work. The Constitutional Convention was organized in 1787 to decide exactly what would be included in this new plan of government, which was seen as necessary after the previous plan for American government, the Articles of Confederation, proved to be too weak. The delegates to the Constitutional Convention agreed to eliminate much of the threat of treason that had traditionally restrained freedom of speech and the press. Only waging war against the United States and "adhering to" (supporting) the nation's enemies would bring charges of treason under the new Constitution.

However, other issues were not agreed upon so easily. Among these were how the government would protect the rights and liberties of citizens. Some in the Constitutional Convention believed that proposed ideas for individual liberty went too far; others felt they did not go far enough to prevent abuses by government.

The Constitution was not ratified by all 13 states until 1789 largely because of these differences and it was only approved after promises were made that rights would soon be added to it. This occurred two years later with the passage of the Bill of Rights.

The process creating the amendments making up the Bill of Rights was among the first duties of the newly formed U.S. Congress. The dozens of ideas considered were eventually narrowed down in the House of Representatives to 17 proposed amendments. The Senate reduced that number to 12 amendments by deleting some and combining other proposed amendments.

"Were it left to me to decide whether we should have a government without newspapers, or newspapers without a government, I should not hesitate a moment to prefer the latter."

—Thomas Jefferson, 1787

THE FEDERALIST PAPERS

The Federalist Papers were written and published during 1787 and 1788 in several New York State newspapers to persuade voters there to ratify the proposed constitution. The 85 essays in the Federalist Papers outline how this new government would operate and why this type of government was the best choice for the United States.

All of the essays were signed with the pen name Publius, but the true identity of the authors has long been a poorly kept secret. Alexander Hamilton and James Madison wrote almost all of the essays, some of which explore early American ideas about freedom of speech and the press.

There was lively debate at the Constitutional Convention over an amendment specifically securing freedom of speech and the press. Virginia delegate James Madison was the leading advocate for this amendment while others, including New York delegate Alexander Hamilton, insisted that it was unnecessary. Hamilton explained that a constitutional guarantee of free speech and free press "depend on public opinion, and on the general spirit of the people and the government." Noah Webster of Connecticut echoed Hamilton's viewpoint, stating that rights to free speech and free press are so obvious that to include them in a constitutional amendment would be like providing all Americans the rights to eat and drink.

In the end, it was Madison's point of view that prevailed. "The freedom of the press and rights of conscience, those choicest privileges of the people, are unguarded in the British Constitution," said Madison, reminding his opponents that these unguarded privileges had been abused for centuries.

For an amendment to be included in the Bill of Rights, three-fourths of the states had to approve them. On December 15, 1791, Virginia became the 10th state to approve 10 of the 12 amendments, making them law. These amendments to the Constitution provided Americans with more guarantees of freedom than any government had ever granted before.

Ratification of the Bill of Rights, 1789–1791

Quebec

claimed by United States and Britain

Maine (Massachusetts)

Lake Superior

Lake Huron

Lake Michigan

New Hampshire
January 25, 1790

Lake Ontario

New York
March 27, 1790

Massachusetts

Rhode Island
June 15, 1790

Lake Erie

Connecticut

Pennsylvania
March 10, 1790

New Jersey
November 20, 1789

Northwest Territory

Delaware
January 28, 1790

Maryland
December 19, 1789

Muskingum R.

Miami R.

Kanawha R.

Ohio R.

Virginia
December 15, 1791

Mississippi R.

Louisiana

ATLANTIC OCEAN

Territory South of the Ohio River

North Carolina
December 22, 1789

South Carolina
January 19, 1790

N

Georgia

Mississippi R.

claimed by Spain, United States, and Georgia

West Florida

East Florida

Gulf of Mexico

United States

U.S. territory

British territory

Spanish territory

Disputed territory

March 10, 1790   Date state ratified Bill of Rights

0   200 miles

0   200 km

Appropriately, it was the First Amendment that provided the most significant liberties. In only 45 words, it protects the free expression of individuals from government interference:

Congress shall make no law respecting an establishment of religion, or prohibiting the free exercise thereof; or abridging the freedom of speech, or of the press; or the right of the people peaceably to assemble, and to petition the government for a redress of grievances.

Led by the First Amendment, the Bill of Rights was now part of a newly expanded and seemingly clearly defined set of freedoms for Americans. But the struggle over exactly how freedom of speech and the press would exist in the United States quickly experienced serious growing pains.

EARLY CHALLENGES TO THE FIRST AMENDMENT

The first major test of the First Amendment's guarantees of free speech and press occurred in 1798, just seven years after its passage. The bitter conflict was between the two main political parties of the time, the Federalists and the Democratic-Republicans, usually referred to as Republicans. The Federalists were led by President John Adams and Alexander Hamilton. They supported a strong centralized government. The Republicans were led by Vice President Thomas Jefferson and James Madison. They believed that a decentralized government that gave more power to states was a better system.

In those days, election rules required that the presidential candidate receiving the second highest amount of votes in the election became vice president, which meant that political rivals Adams and Jefferson, who were supposed to be working together, actually disagreed on many important issues. One of these issues was America's policy on a war between France and Great Britain that began in 1793. President Adams and most Federalists supported Great Britain, while Vice President Jefferson and the Republicans tended to favor the French. As time went on, relations between the U.S. and French governments became tense, particularly following French attacks on U.S. shipping.

By 1798, the hostility between the two main American political parties was reaching its peak. Federalists often accused Republicans of siding with the French. Republicans, with hopes of promoting Jefferson for president in the 1800 election, responded by attacking President Adams and other Federalists in speeches and newspaper articles.

This made the Federalists, who enjoyed a majority in the U.S. Congress, furious. Explaining that the First Amendment was not intended to protect what they believed was a vicious, dishonest, and irresponsible press that damaged people's reputations, the Federalists pushed through the Alien and Sedition Acts of 1798.

The Alien Act was mainly aimed at French and Irish immigrants, many of whom supported the Republicans. This act allowed the government to arrest and deport any foreigner judged "dangerous to America's peace and safety." Although the act was never enforced, it did cause fear among many immigrants, who often went into hiding or fled the country.

The Sedition Act, though, was enforced. This law made it a crime to write, print, utter, or publish "any false, scandalous, and malicious criticism . . . against the government of the United States . . . Congress . . . or the . . . President." It also made it illegal to "incite against them the hatred of the good people of the United States." Offenders of the Sedition Act were subject to fines of up to 2,000 dollars and imprisonment for up to two years.

Opinions over the meaning of freedom of speech and the press, which had been relatively mild during the creation of the Bill of Rights, now became very heated. Federalists explained that the First Amendment should only apply to truthful, responsible, and reasonable differences of opinion and that the Sedition Act would not punish those kinds of expression. They responded to criticism that this law resembled the hated English law of seditious libel that had been fought during colonial times by saying that the Sedition Act did not promote censorship or require prior approval of expression and that it upheld the standard established at the trial of John Peter Zenger that only false criticism could be punished.

OPPOSITION TO THE
ALIEN AND SEDITION ACTS

Opponents of the Sedition Act countered these arguments with vigorous protest. They wondered if the "false criticism" prohibited in the Sedition Act would really mean any criticism the Federalists did

> "To the press alone, checkered as it is with abuses, the world is indebted for all the triumphs which have been gained by reason and humanity over error and oppression."
>
> —James Madison, 1798

not like. Thomas Jefferson called it an unconstitutional "reign of terror," and James Madison drafted a resolution describing it as: "a power not delegated by the Constitution, but, on the contrary, expressly and positively forbidden by one of the amendments thereto,—a power which, more than any other, ought to produce universal alarm, because it is leveled against the right of freely examining public characters and measures, and of free communication among the people thereon, which has ever been justly deemed the only effectual guardian of every other right."

Eventually, 25 men, mostly editors of pro-Republican newspapers, were arrested for "treasonable" activities under the authority of the Sedition Act. Ten of them were convicted and their newspapers were forced to close. But the most famous prosecution for violation of the Sedition Act was the first one—targeting Vermont congressman Matthew Lyon. In a letter to a Vermont newspaper, Lyon accused President Adams of greed and selfishness. Lyon was convicted, fined $1,000, and forced to serve four months in jail.

An indication of the public's opposition to the Sedition Act was seen when Lyon was reelected to Congress while still in jail. In the presidential election of 1800, Thomas Jefferson easily defeated John Adams, partially because of how many Americans feared and disliked the Federalist-supported Sedition Act. Once he became president, Jefferson quickly pardoned those convicted under the Sedition Act and, although Federalists still controlled Congress, no

THE TRAGIC END TO THE MAN ON THE $10 BILL

Alexander Hamilton was one of the most influential of the American founding fathers. He was an officer in the Continental army, which defeated the British in the Revolutionary War, and he later became the first U.S. secretary of the treasury. After he left government, he continued to be an active and important leader in the development of the young nation, including his advocacy of freedom of the press in *The People v. Croswell*.

However, just a few months after the conclusion of this case, Hamilton was challenged to a duel by his political rival Aaron Burr. At the duel, Hamilton reportedly fired into the air while Burr took direct aim, hitting Hamilton with a shot that would result in his death the following day.

attempt was made to renew the law when it expired in 1801. Eventually, Congress ordered all fines paid under the law to be returned.

In Jefferson's first inaugural address, he expressed his belief in the value of free expression by saying that if anyone wanted to dissolve the government of the United States or change its form, he could speak freely. But soon, Jefferson was seeking to suppress criticism and opposition in heavy-handed and, many felt, unfair, ways. Because the First Amendment restricted only the federal government, Jefferson encouraged state governments to enact libel laws that still often prohibited even truthful criticism.

Using these state laws, the Jefferson administration arrested many of his critics. In the 1804 New York case *The People v. Croswell,* defense lawyer Alexander Hamilton argued that truth should be a defense in state libel cases. Although Hamilton lost that case, his reasoning helped persuade New York and soon many more states to enact laws allowing truth as a defense against charges of libel.

James Madison, often called the "Father of the Constitution," was the fourth president of the United States. *(Library of Congress, Prints and Photographs Division [LC-USZ62-13004])*

James Madison followed Thomas Jefferson as president and strengthened his legacy as a champion of free expression. During the War of 1812 with Great Britain, many opponents of Madison's policies openly criticized him. Some supporters of the president feared that their criticism would harm or even destroy the country, but Madison consistently refused to use his power to silence them. The United States won the War of 1812, and Madison was reelected to another term as president in 1812. His example of tolerance for dissenting opinions, both written and spoken, helped the emerging freedoms of speech and the press mature and become stronger.

Controversy over the limits of free speech and a free press would continue, but as the United States entered the 19th century, traditions allowing criticism of government and public officials were increasingly becoming a well-established foundation of American life.

"I contend for the liberty of publishing truth, with good motives and for justifiable ends, even though it reflect on government, magistrates, or private persons."

—*Alexander Hamilton, 1804*

3

Influencing American
Society in the 19th Century

The 19th century in the United States was a time of sweeping and often difficult change. Immigration from Europe and industrial development led to a population boom in major cities. Debates over slavery grew steadily, leading to an influential abolitionist movement and eventually to a bloody civil war. These events and others that occurred during the 1800s were all in some way inspired by or reflected by evolving understandings of the First Amendment's freedoms of speech and the press.

THE RISE OF AMERICAN NEWSPAPERS

Most newspapers in the early 19th century enjoyed almost limitless freedom to criticize public officials, though exceptions were typically made during wartime. For the most part, the government encouraged the spread of information to the public by offering inexpensive postal rates for newspapers. This allowed people with little money to publish small newspapers and it helped the poor afford to buy them.

With more readers, publishers were able to make money through the sale of advertising. Boosted by the profits and wide freedoms of the press, the newspaper industry continued to grow and become more competitive. In 1833, a young printer named Benjamin Day began publishing the *New York Sun*, which sold for only a penny. The *Sun* covered political news and important events in the city, and it was the first newspaper to report on police news.

The success of the *Sun* prompted other papers to find innovative ways to attract readers. Newspapers began producing even more lively stories and broader features, such as society, financial,

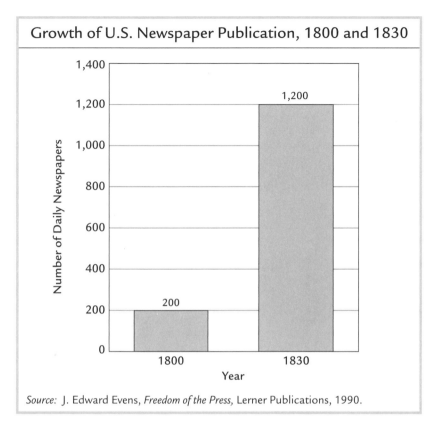

Growth of U.S. Newspaper Publication, 1800 and 1830

Source: J. Edward Evens, *Freedom of the Press,* Lerner Publications, 1990.

Advanced technology, increased urban populations, and rising wealth and literacy rates helped spur growth in U.S. newspaper circulation between 1800 and 1830.

and sports articles. Throughout all the changes taking place in the newspaper industry, papers remained a common and powerful voice for political opinion, particularly in the editorial pages. This was most obvious regarding the increasingly volatile topic of slavery.

THE POWER OF ABOLITIONIST SPEECH AND PRESS

At the beginning of the 19th century, those who called for an end to slavery, or *abolitionists,* were few and they were located almost entirely in the North, where the practice of forced labor without pay no longer existed. By the 1830s, however, the abolitionist movement was gaining momentum. In the Missouri Compromise

"I am in earnest—I will not equivocate—I will not excuse—I will not retreat a single inch—and I will be heard!"

—*William Lloyd Garrison, inaugural issue of* The Liberator, *1831*

of 1820, antislavery forces in Congress ensured that territory in northern areas added to the United States by the huge addition of land from the Louisiana Purchase would remain free of slavery.

Encouraged by the success of white abolitionists, some blacks sought to fight slavery through organized revolts, and they often used pamphlets to help spread their ideas. Among these men was David Walker. Walker was a free black living in Boston in 1829 when he wrote his *Appeal,* urging slaveholders to repent for their sins and trying to inspire active uprisings by slaves. When copies of the *Appeal* were found by authorities in North Carolina and elsewhere in the South, many slaveholders panicked. The Georgia state

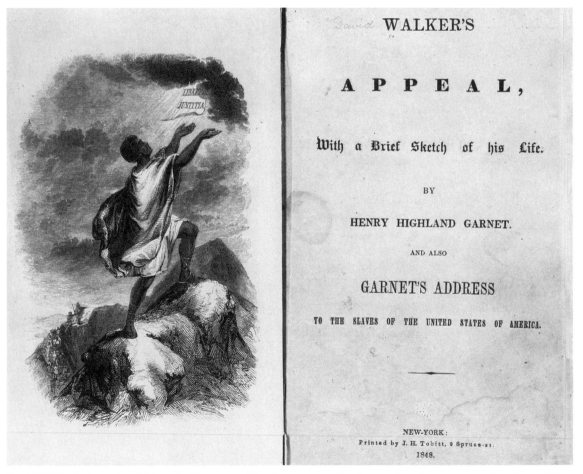

David Walker's *Appeal*—which called for an end to slavery—was the focus of controversy over freedom of the press. *(Library of Congress, Prints and Photographs Division [LC-USZ62-105530])*

legislature rushed through a law requiring the death penalty for "circulation of pamphlets of evil tendency." The mayor of Savannah, Georgia, wrote to Boston mayor Harrison Gray Otis, asking him to punish Walker. While Otis condemned the pamphlet, he explained that Walker had not broken any Massachusetts law. Walker died a year after the publication of his *Appeal,* a death many thought was the result of poison.

In 1831, Massachusetts abolitionist William Lloyd Garrison published the first copies of *The Liberator,* a paper filled with sharp criticism of slavery and slaveholders. Although Garrison advocated nonviolence, he published Walker's *Appeal,* and some southern papers began to inform their readers of Garrison's words. That same year, escaped slave Nat Turner led the most widespread slave revolt in the South, in which 60 whites were killed before it was ended. Virginia governor John Floyd expressed the feelings of many when he placed some of the blame for the revolt on the influence of *The Liberator* and other abolitionist newspapers.

Vocal debate about slavery was also increasing in the South during the early 1830s. The Virginia state legislature debated a resolution for the abolition of slavery that failed by a vote of 73 to 48. Most of those who supported abolition

Frederick Douglass is shown fighting off an angry mob opposed to his speech arguing for an end to slavery. *(Library of Congress, Prints and Photographs Division [LC-USZ62-76079])*

explained their views using social or economic reasons, not moral ones, and many of these legislators were not reelected because of their opposition to slavery.

The close-call victory for slaveholders in the Virginia legislature led to intense efforts to protect slavery from printed and spoken attacks. Many southern states enacted laws against abolitionist ideas, such as North Carolina's prohibition of publications that "excite insurrection, conspiracy or resistance in the slaves, free negroes, or persons of colour within the state." Southern states dug in even more against abolition in 1833 when the U.S. Supreme Court ruled in *Barron v. Baltimore* that guarantees in the Bill of Rights were intended to limit the powers of the federal government and did not apply to states.

Efforts by southern supporters of slavery did not discourage abolitionists. It actually seemed to motivate them even more. In 1833, the first national abolitionist organization was founded, the American Anti-Slavery Society. It targeted freedom for slaves

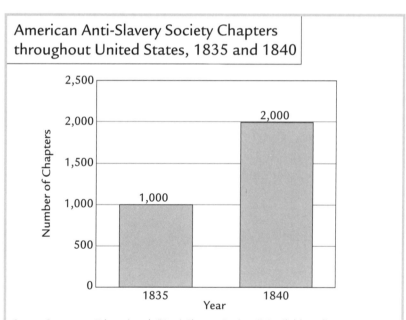

American Anti-Slavery Society Chapters throughout United States, 1835 and 1840

Source: Spartacus Educational, "Anti-Slavery Society." Available online. URL: http://www.spartacus.Schoolnet.co.uk/USAantislavery.htm. Downloaded on September 10, 2004, and The Free Dictionary.com, "American Anti-Slavery Society." Available online. URL: http://encyclopedia. the free dictionary.com/American%20Anti-Slavery%20Society. Downloaded on September 10, 2004.

In 1831, brothers Arthur and Lewis Tappan established the first antislavery society in New York. Organized meetings, printed publications, and lecture tours quickly led to enormous growth of the movement to end slavery.

largely through changing public opinion, believing that as southerners were persuaded that slavery was a sin, the practice would
be stopped by individual action or state laws.

Abolitionists traveled throughout the North to speak against
slavery, and they took advantage of cheap printing and the wealth
of their supporters to flood the country with antislavery literature.
Starting with a few societies in the early 1830s, they grew to more
than 1,000 groups by 1837. In response, their opponents increased
calls for the suppression of abolitionism, raising questions about
the meaning of free speech and free press.

As abolitionist societies grew in number and power, the reactions
against their demands for an immediate end to slavery provided

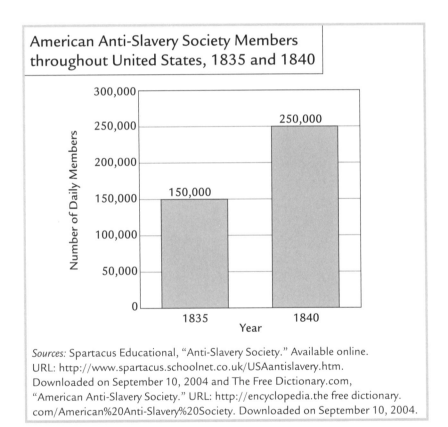

American Anti-Slavery Society Members throughout United States, 1835 and 1840

Sources: Spartacus Educational, "Anti-Slavery Society." Available online.
URL: http://www.spartacus.schoolnet.co.uk/USAantislavery.htm.
Downloaded on September 10, 2004 and The Free Dictionary.com,
"American Anti-Slavery Society." URL: http://encyclopedia.the free dictionary.
com/American%20Anti-Slavery%20Society. Downloaded on September 10, 2004.

Despite sometimes violent opposition to their activities, antislavery societies
enjoyed a boom in membership. The American Anti-Slavery Society was
formally dissolved in 1870 after the Civil War and emancipation of
American slaves.

a strong reaction in the North and the South. In fact, most antiabolitionist conflict took place in the North, as this is where almost all antiabolitionist speeches and meetings occurred. There were many cases of mob action against abolition meetings between 1833 and 1837, including an 1835 incident in which Garrison was led around Boston with a rope around his neck.

At the same time as mob action against those speaking out and writing against slavery grew in the North, official southern suppression of antislavery expression grew in the South. In 1836, a Virginia law criminalized antislavery statements that just a few years earlier were expressed on the floor of its legislature. Southerners were especially angry about the often successful attempts by northern abolitionists to send materials through the mail into southern states. With President Andrew Jackson's support, the Post Office Act of 1836 was passed, allowing states to refuse to deliver certain mail, such as abolitionist newspapers and pamphlets.

The harsh rejection of debate on slavery in the South and the intolerance and mob action against abolitionists in the North led in some cases to a backlash of sympathy for the cause of slavery. Many northerners opposed slavery but supported the southern states' rights to have it. Even though these northerners disliked abolitionist "agitation," they rarely felt that laws should be put in place to prevent the rights of abolitionists to speak or publish their beliefs.

Many southern lawmakers wanted their northern counterparts to legally suppress antislavery speech and press, arguing that it threatened to ignite slave rebellion and undermine the strength of the nation. But northern reluctance to do this was based in the value of the freedom of speech and the press. This was explained by Pennsylvania governor George Wolf, who said:

> . . . [The] crusade against slavery is the offspring of fanaticism of the most dangerous and alarming character, which if not speedily checked may kindle a fire which it may require the best blood of the country to quench . . . [but] legislation cannot be brought to bear upon it without endangering other rights and privileges . . . The freedom of speech and of the press, which after all is the safeguard to free discussion . . . must not be infringed upon or controlled . . . to remedy some temporary mischief only.

GROWING TENSION DIVIDES THE NATION

The brewing turmoil over abolition expression sunk to a tragic low in 1837, when Elijah Lovejoy, editor of the Illinois abolitionist paper *The Alton Observer,* was killed while defending his printing press from an antiabolitionist mob. Lovejoy was a 35-year-old Presbyterian minister who had long railed against the evils of slavery. He had already had three printing presses destroyed by mobs, and his requests to authorities for protection from threats were repeatedly ignored. His defense of his printing press and murder made him a martyr for free speech and free press to many throughout the country who learned of his killing in newspaper accounts.

After Lovejoy's murder, public opinion against mob violence directed at those who wrote or spoke out against slavery soared. The line between abolitionists and those who supported their rights and privileges to free speech and press and their opponents became even wider. An editorial from New Hampshire's *Nashua Courier* noted: "It matters not whether Lovejoy acted prudently or imprudently—morally right or wrong. He was in the exercise of a right guaranteed by the laws, and under their protection . . . while we retain the name of freemen, we will speak and publish our opinions boldly—we will have a government of laws, and not the despotism of a mob."

> "Those who profess to favor freedom, and yet depreciate agitation, are men who want crops without plowing up the ground. They want rain without thunder and lightning."
>
> —*Frederick Douglass, 1857*

FREDERICK DOUGLASS
Great American Speaker

As a nine-year-old slave, Frederick Douglass (then named Frederick Bailey) was secretly taught to read by the wife of his master. Four years later he bought a book featuring a collection of great speeches, *The Columbian Orator* by Caleb Bingham, and used it to strengthen his reading and speaking skills.

At age 20, Douglass escaped from slavery in Maryland and moved to New York, then Massachusetts, where he attracted attention during a speech about his life as a slave. For the next two decades, Douglass spoke tirelessly against slavery and published a celebrated biography and an abolitionist newspaper, *The North Star.* During the Civil War, Douglass's speeches and writings helped recruit black troops, including his own sons, into the Union army, and he also served as an adviser to President Abraham Lincoln.

"Where slavery is there can be no free speech, no free thought, no free press, no regard for constitutions . . ."

—Michigan congressman Henry Waldon, 1860

Over the course of the next few decades, the cause of abolition became stronger, and so did southern resistance to it. The issue of slavery became even more urgent following the 1854 Kansas-Nebraska Act, which repealed the Missouri Compromise by making the decision of slavery in newly added territory the choice of voters in those regions, and the 1857 *Dred Scott* decision by the U.S. Supreme Court, which ruled that enslaved blacks remained the property of their owners even when they were on free soil.

Free speech and free press contributed enormously to this period of heightened tension, particularly the powerful oratory of black abolitionist Frederick Douglass, the best-selling novel *Uncle Tom's Cabin* by Harriet Beecher Stowe, and Hinton Helper's nonfiction book *The Impending Crisis*. Publishing these speeches and books in the South often led to harsh reprisal from legal authorities and mobs of private citizens.

Alongside the critical question of abolition was a continued concern for the protection of the First Amendment rights of freedom of speech and the press. Criticizing the arrests of distributors of *The Impending Crisis,* Ohio congressman Sidney Edgerton said, "Gentlemen of the South, the North demands of you the observance of constitutional obligations . . . She demands the freedom of speech and of the press; and if your peculiar institution [slavery] cannot stand before them, let it go down."

FREE SPEECH AND PRESS DURING THE CIVIL WAR AND RECONSTRUCTION

The passions and fears of the Civil War, fought between 1861 and 1865, presented serious and complex threats to freedom of speech and the press. Southern states, which had seceded from the Union, were not under the authority of the U.S. government. But those in the North who were suspected of being involved, or about to be involved, in disloyalty or treason were often arrested and convicted under tougher wartime laws. There were an estimated 38,000 of these arrests. Many critics of President Abraham Lincoln's effort to fight the South in order to preserve the Union kept quiet to avoid fines or prison.

President Lincoln was troubled by the limits he enforced on free expression, but he reasoned that they were necessary during such a dangerous time. Under Lincoln's order, some newspapers in the North were shut down by Union military commanders and the postmaster banned the mailing of a number of newspapers. Lincoln claimed, much as later presidents during wartime would, that he had to jail those suspected of treason because of their threat to national security.

One important Civil War–era case involving the freedom of press was that of *Newark* (New Jersey) *Evening Journal* editor E. M. Fuller, who was arrested and fined on charges of inciting insurrection and discouraging enlistments in the army. In the editorial that led to his arrest, Fuller wrote, "It will be seen that Mr. Lincoln has called for another half million of men. Those who wish to be butchered will please step forward. All others will please stay home and defy old Abe and his minions to drag them from their families."

Other attempts by Lincoln to suppress freedom of speech and the press resulted in strong outcries of opposition. The 1863 arrest of former Ohio congressman and Civil War critic Clement Vallandigham led to his conviction for disloyalty and banishment from the United States. Later that year, the *Chicago Times* newspaper was shut down for repeatedly publishing articles viewed as aiding the rebellion. Opposition to these actions was strong, and within months the *Chicago Times* was allowed to continue publishing.

Critics of President Lincoln argued that the rights to freedom of speech and the press during the Civil War were weakened, while his supporters pointed out that with the situation he faced, he had responded reasonably. Despite the restrictions on expression that occurred, Lincoln's political opponents were largely allowed to continue their verbal and written attacks, and free elections were held in which the candidates openly criticized each other and the government. The high regard Americans had for freedom of speech and the press was showing signs of growth, even in the midst of the Civil War, which helped keep suppression of these cherished rights limited.

In 1868, three years after the end of the Civil War, the Fourteenth Amendment to the Constitution was ratified. Section I of that amendment stated:

> *All persons born or naturalized in the United States, and subject to the jurisdiction thereof, are citizens of the United States and of the state wherein they reside. No state shall make or enforce any law which shall abridge the privileges or immunities of citizens of the*

> "Must I shoot a simple-minded soldier boy who deserts, while I must not touch a hair of a wily agitator who induced him to desert?"
>
> —*President Abraham Lincoln, 1863*

United States; nor shall any state deprive any person of life, liberty, or property, without due process of law; nor deny to any person within its jurisdiction the equal protection of the laws.

The amendment's most important legacy to protection of freedom of speech and the press was the way it prohibited state governments from infringing on free expression rights the same way the First Amendment prevented the trampling of these rights by the federal government. This measure of "double security" was intended to protect individual citizens while allowing states to create laws that complied with the U.S. Constitution.

But in the readmitted southern states, now without the presence of federal troops that were there during the post–Civil War Reconstruction, restrictions on the rights of blacks continued. Though no longer slaves and now supported by new laws preventing state restrictions of their rights, blacks were routinely suppressed through codes and custom from enjoying the full rights that they were entitled to as American citizens. Groups such as the Ku Klux Klan regularly intimidated blacks for saying or publishing their beliefs. This led to a struggle between federal and state governments over respect for individual rights, including those of speech and press, that would continue for more than 100 years, reappearing as a focus of the Civil Rights movement of the 1960s.

INCREASING CONCERN WITH "OUTSIDERS"

Another group of people who were sometimes excluded from the protections of the First Amendment were those often considered "outsiders"—including immigrants, workers trying to organize labor unions, and people with radical political beliefs.

A fatal example of this was the reaction to the 1886 bomb explosion at Chicago's Haymarket Square. The night after a confrontation between striking workers and their replacements near the McCormick Harvest Company's plant, *anarchists* (people who believe that all forms of government should be abolished) organized a rally at Haymarket Square to support the strikers. When the police moved to break up the demonstration, a bomb exploded. An exchange of gunfire followed, resulting in 18 deaths and more than 100 injuries.

A riot in Chicago's Haymarket Square resulted in 18 deaths and a crackdown on free expression. *(Library of Congress, Prints and Photographs Division [LC-USZ62-796])*

The person who threw the bomb was never discovered, but police arrested eight anarchists who were then tried for murder. Even though five of them had not been at the Haymarket rally, the government argued that because they advocated violence in their speeches and writings, they were responsible for the murders. All eight men were convicted and four of them were hanged. Three of them were later pardoned by the governor of Illinois.

YELLOW JOURNALISM

As the 19th century was coming to a close, the influence of freedom of speech and the press was increasing in the daily lives of Americans. Industrialization turned small towns into busy big cities, and the demand for newspapers in these cities grew as well. With this rising demand came fierce competition among newspapers. Some papers tried to boost sales by turning away from previously held standards

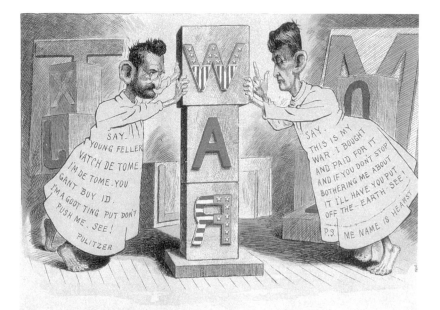

THE BIG TYPE WAR OF THE YELLOW KIDS.

The journalistic recklessness of leading newspaper publishers Joseph Pulitzer and William Randolph Hearst during the Spanish-American War era is criticized in this cartoon. The caption accompanying the image read, "They are amusing cusses. War news comes in and they both claim to have seen it first." *(Library of Congress, Prints and Photographs Division [LC-USZC4-3800])*

toward sensationalism, intended to provoke quick, sharp, and often superficial emotion in the reader.

Two leaders of sensationalism were newspaper publishers Joseph Pulitzer and William Randolph Hearst. Pulitzer's *New York World* and Hearst's *New York Journal* waged battle in the late 1890s, highlighting an irresponsible style of reporting known as "yellow journalism" because of the yellow ink used by the papers in their comic sections. These papers featured bold, "screaming" headlines announcing crime, scandal, and gossip, and sometimes included false interviews and fake pictures.

The effects of yellow journalism peaked just before the Spanish-American War in 1898. Both the *New York Journal* and the *New York World* enjoyed increased sales following reports of atrocities committed by Spanish forces in Cuba. Hearst even assigned a reporter to provide sketches of Cuban resistance to the Spanish. When the reporter informed Hearst that there was no fighting to

JOSEPH PULITZER
From Yellow Journalism to Prestigious Awards

Joseph Pulitzer was born into a wealthy Hungarian family in 1847. He came to the United States in 1864 and within 10 years began building his fortune in newspaper publishing. The success of his *St. Louis Post-Dispatch* led Pulitzer to purchase the struggling *New York World* newspaper. Under Pulitzer's leadership, the circulation of the *World* grew from 15,000 in 1883 to 150,000 in 1888, making it the most popular newspaper in the United States. But Pulitzer was also criticized by many for the sensationalistic coverage of national and world events in the paper.

Upon his death in 1911, Pulitzer left funds to establish a school of journalism at Columbia University in New York City and to endow the Pulitzer Prizes, which are awarded for distinguished work in journalism, literature, and music and are widely considered to be among the most prestigious honors given to members of the press.

report, Hearst replied, "You provide the pictures and I'll provide the war!"

When the U.S. battleship *Maine* exploded and sank in the harbor of Havana, Cuba, on February 15, 1898, many newspapers, especially those that featured sensationalist stories, blamed Spain, even though there was little evidence to support this accusation. But big headlines and even bigger sales followed as the United States soon declared war on Spain and then won the Spanish-American War.

Soon, distaste for some of the abuses of yellow journalism led to the creation of journalistic associations, which created codes of conduct and ethics. Sensationalism still existed, but more Americans than ever before were realizing the responsibilities that come with the rights to freedom of speech and the press.

Americans now had more than a century of experience dealing with the benefits and conflicts of free expression. But as the 20th century began, these battles were expanding, and in many ways, just beginning.

4

Evolving Roles in the Early 20th Century

The first half of the 1900s was a period of exciting and often frightening change in the United States. During these years, Americans experienced two world wars, major social reform, and rapid technological and industrial change. During this time, the freedoms of speech and the press continued to play a growing role in American life, even as the power of these rights shifted under the pressures of dramatic events at home and abroad.

FIGHTING RADICAL IDEAS WITH LEGISLATION

The 20th century, which began with so much optimism in the United States, quickly witnessed tragedy in September 1901 when President William McKinley was assassinated. McKinley's killer was a young man named Leon Czolgosz. Although he was born in the United States, Czolgosz was the son of Polish immigrants, and he was identified by many Americans as part of the anarchist movement, which was heavily influenced by recent European immigrants.

Czolgosz was tried, convicted, and executed for McKinley's murder. Also, as a result of the assassination, there was a wave of laws passed aimed at restricting the free expression of anarchists and the foreign-born.

Sedition laws, similar to the Alien and Sedition Acts more than 100 years earlier, were passed in various states. In 1903, Congress passed an immigration act that for the first time prohibited entry into the United States of certain immigrants based on their associations and beliefs.

Opposition to the demands and influence of labor unions is shown in this cartoon from 1914. *(Library of Congress, Prints and Photographs Division [LC-USZ62-68685])*

Those concerned about the expression of radical ideas also focused their attention on the slowly but steadily growing labor movement in the United States. The largest and most visible group of laborers was the Industrial Workers of the World (IWW), also known as the Wobblies. The IWW attracted and organized many workers that other unions often did not want, such as women, blacks, southern and eastern European immigrants, and other ethnic minorities, including Mexicans and Asians.

The Wobblies relied on their rights to freedom of speech and the press to explain their views and increase their following. But the more successful they became, the more opposition to them grew. Statements from IWW leaders such as "We shall conquer the world for the working class" and "We are the modern abolitionists fighting against wage slavery" worried many political and business leaders. Realizing that the IWW needed speeches and writings for their growth, these leaders passed local laws that severely restricted the Wobblies' ability to stand on a soapbox and make open-air speeches and to freely distribute their literature.

The Wobblies fought these new laws in court and sometimes were successful in getting them overturned. But this success came at a high price, including arrests, beatings, and expensive legal battles. There was also much opposition to the Wobblies from local citizens, though many others admired their tenacious defense of free expression, even if they rejected their political views.

The IWW's powerful rise and influence on American society was severely damaged by the opposition to people perceived as radicals that escalated in the United States during World War I and immediately afterward (1917–20). The main instrument used to repress free speech and press during this time was the Espionage Act of 1917. This law was designed to discourage and punish those who during wartime ". . . make or convey false reports or false statements with intent to interfere with the operation or success of the military or naval forces of the United States or to promote the success of its enemies and . . . cause or attempt to cause insubordination, disloyalty, mutiny, refusal of duty, in the military or naval forces of the United States, or . . . obstruct the recruiting or enlistment service of the United States." Punishment included a fine of up to $10,000, imprisonment for as many as 20 years, or both.

Still, there were many people who believed that the punishments for violations of the Espionage Act did not go far enough to ensure loyalty during wartime. They believed that people who said the United States was wrong to fight in the war were disloyal and that such disloyalty was dangerous, requiring stricter penalties.

A majority of the Congress agreed with this argument and passed the Sedition Act in 1918. Among the activities prohibited during wartime under this law were saying, writing, or publishing anything considered disloyal, profane, or abusive about the U.S. government, the flag, or military uniforms. The Sedition Act of 1918 also made it a crime to support country at war with the United States. Supporters of the Espionage and Sedition acts were pleased with their results.

Eventually, more than 2,000 people were convicted and sentenced to jail time for violations of these laws, and countless others kept their criticism of the U.S. role in World War I quiet.

However, disapproval of the Espionage and Sedition acts grew as these laws were increasingly applied to punish speech and writing that criticized not only the war effort but the U.S. government as well. Many people thought that any criticism of the government or a particular goal of the government harmed the war effort. As a result, people were sometimes jailed for things that did not seem disloyal to many people at the time. Examples include a man who was arrested for suggesting that the government raise taxes instead of selling war bonds, and a Minnesota man who told a group of women that no soldier would ever see the socks they were knitting. Even criticism of nongovernment organizations that had a hand in the war effort, such as the Red Cross and YMCA, could lead to arrest.

Spoken words were not the only focus of the Espionage and Sedition acts during World War I. Written words were as well. The Post Office used the authority of the Trading with the Enemy Act of 1917 to require certified translations of foreign language newspapers, particularly those in German, which were sometimes sympathetic to America's World War I enemy Germany. By the end of World War I, about half of the German-language newspapers in the United States had stopped publishing. The Post Office also restricted the distribution of socialist newspapers, and some other publications were only allowed to continue if they agreed to print nothing about the war.

THE U.S. SUPREME COURT PLAYS A LARGER ROLE

During this period, the courts—particularly the U.S. Supreme Court—became more active in trying to clarify the power and boundaries of American citizens' rights to free expression. The first major Supreme Court case concerning possible free speech violations of the Espionage and Sedition acts was *Schenck v. United States* in 1919. This case concerned Charles Schenck, an official with the Socialist Party, who wrote and distributed a pamphlet that stated that the World War I military draft was unconstitutional and that those who were drafted should resist induction into the armed forces in any legal way possible. He was found guilty under the

Sedition Act of trying to cause disobedience in the armed forces and for attempting to disrupt military recruiting.

In the unanimous Supreme Court ruling upholding Schenck's conviction, Justice Oliver Wendell Holmes explained in the majority opinion that there are circumstances in which individual rights to free speech may be denied:

> We admit that in many places and in ordinary times the defendants in saying all that was said in the circular would have been within their constitutional rights. But the character of every act depends upon the circumstances in which it is done. The most stringent protection of free speech would not protect a man in falsely shouting fire in a theatre and causing a panic.

Holmes went on to address the rights to free expression during wartime, asserting: "When a nation is at war many things that might be said in time of peace are such a hindrance to its effort that their utterance will not be endured so long as men fight and that no Court could regard them as protected by any constitutional right."

The Supreme Court's decision in *Schenck* established a test to help clarify what kind of expression would be allowed. In what would become known as the "clear and present danger" test, Holmes wrote, "The question in every case is whether the words used are used in such circumstances and are of such a nature as to create a clear and present danger that they will bring about the substantive evils that Congress has a right to prevent."

The following year the Supreme Court again tried to draw appropriate guidelines for free expression in the case of *Abrams v. United States*. In a 7-2 ruling, the Court upheld the conviction of five young Russian immigrants who had distributed pamphlets protesting the U.S. decision to send troops to Russia during the Russian Revolution. This ruling also produced another test for figuring out the proper limits of free expression known as the "dangerous tendency" test. This test asked: Could the words of the speaker or writer start an action that could endanger public peace or national security?

But the justices who disagreed with the majority's decision, Oliver Wendell Holmes and Louis Brandeis, provided encouragement for those who hoped to see more individual freedom of speech and press. In his dissent, Holmes wrote: ". . . I think that we should be eternally vigilant against attempts to check the expression of opinions that we loathe and believe to be fraught with

"... the best test of truth is the power of the thought to get itself accepted in the competition of the market . . ."

—*Supreme Court Justice Oliver Wendell Holmes, 1920*

death, unless they so imminently threaten immediate interference with the lawful and pressing purposes of the law that an immediate check is required to save the country."

THE RED SCARE AND PALMER RAIDS

Even after World War I ended and victorious American soldiers returned home, wartime restrictions on freedom of speech and the press remained. Now much of the United States was gripped by the "Red Scare"—a fear of socialist and communist influence—that followed the communist revolution in Russia and the continued concern with radicals, foreigners, and labor leaders. U.S. Attorney General A. Mitchell Palmer expressed the fear of many when he warned: "The chief evil of the Red [communist] movement, both here and abroad, consists in the fact that it accomplishes a constant spread of a disease of evil thinking."

Palmer's most lasting legacy to this Red Scare period would be raids—often referred to as "Palmer Raids"—carried out on suspected leaders and participants in radical causes. The most sweeping of these raids were conducted on January 2, 1920, and resulted in the arrests of more than 4,000 radicals in more than 30 cities. Four days later another series of raids led to the arrests of over 6,000 more people, mostly immigrants involved in the labor movement or political groups.

Although most Americans initially supported the Palmer Raids, many others were outraged by what they believed was the reckless

THE PALMER RAIDS AND J. EDGAR HOOVER

In 1919 Attorney General A. Mitchell Palmer recruited a young man named J. Edgar Hoover to be his special assistant. Hoover impressed his boss with his effort and ability in using the Espionage and Sedition acts to prosecute suspected radicals during the Palmer Raids.

At age 29, Hoover became the head of the Federal Bureau of Investigation (FBI), the top national law enforcement agency. Hoover served in that capacity until he died almost 48 years later. During this time, Hoover was one of the most powerful men in the United States. He used his position to collect information on a wide range of people, including prominent politicians and leading critics of government.

U.S. Attorney General A. Mitchell Palmer, architect of the Palmer Raids of 1919–20, is shown in this cartoon as the jailer of labor union leader Eugene V. Debs, who was serving time in jail for sedition when he received almost 1 million votes in the 1920 presidential election. *(Courtesy of BoondocksNet.com)*

and unconstitutional way the raids were conducted. Mass arrests often left homes and offices ransacked and included the confiscation of personal literature and letters on what was often later proved to be flimsy or inaccurate evidence of disloyalty.

By the early 1920s, the Red Scare had eased as Americans saw that communism had not spread throughout Europe and labor unrest at home had cooled down. Controversial speech and writing also decreased because of the intimidation caused by the crackdown on radical activities and the vocal protest against the Palmer Raids by some prominent Americans. The Espionage and Sedition acts were repealed by Congress in 1921, and growing numbers of Americans became increasingly concerned that the "clear and present danger" test and "dangerous tendency" test gave the government too much power to regulate free speech and press. Concern over the government's crackdown on free expression during the Red Scare, which peaked with the Palmer Raids, led to the formation in 1920 of the American Civil Liberties Union (ACLU), a private organization dedicated to defending the guarantees listed in the Bill of Rights. The ACLU remains a very influential and controversial organization involved in battles of free expression.

Restrictions on free speech and free press continued to ease throughout the 1920s. Although the 1925 Supreme Court case *Gitlow v. United States* upheld the conviction of a writer advocating communism, the decision did expand protection of individuals' rights to expression from interference from states. Now the Supreme Court became the undisputed focus for arguments on free expression.

Evidence that the Supreme Court and American society had developed more permissive views on free expression was the 1927

THE ACLU
At the Center of the Storm

Like other founders of the American Civil Liberties Union (ACLU), Roger Baldwin was concerned that the Bill of Rights was nothing but a parchment barrier to governmental abuse. "Silence never won rights," said Baldwin, "They are not handed down from above; they are forced by pressures from below."

The ACLU has traditionally been involved in the most controversial legal cases, defending a wide range of groups, including some, such as the Ku Klux Klan, whose views few support. The ACLU explains that it does not defend these groups because it agrees with their ideology, but because it believes in their basic freedom to express themselves as they choose.

"The greatest dangers to liberty lurk in the insidious encroachment by men of zeal, well-meaning but without understanding."

—*Supreme Court Justice Louis Brandeis, 1928*

case *Near v. Minnesota*. This case centered on a 1925 Minnesota "gag" law that prohibited the publication of obscene, scandalous writings that were often harmful to someone's reputation. That law had been used to obtain a restraining order against a small Minneapolis paper, *The Saturday Press*, which frequently included racial slurs, vicious criticism of the police, and other unsupported accusations against public officials.

In a 5-4 decision, the Supreme Court held in favor of the publisher, explaining, "[T]he fact that the liberty of the press may be abused by miscreant purveyors of scandal does not make any the less necessary the immunity of the press from previous restraint." In other words, the public's right to have access to opinion without government interference was so important that it was even guaranteed to those who used their free expression rights irresponsibly.

THE MUCKRAKERS

Freedom of the press was also strengthened during the first part of the 20th century by the powerful influence of journalists known as muckrakers. President Theodore Roosevelt gave them their name in 1906 when he referred to an old story of a man, "muckrake in hand," who collected dirt rather than pursue other interests. Roosevelt recognized the muckrakers' important role in exposing social,

This 1907 newspaper cartoon criticizes the employers and effects of child labor. *(Library of Congress, Prints and Photographs Division [LC-USZ62-55984])*

political, and economic problems in America's increasingly industrial society, but he worried that sometimes these writers went too far in stirring up radical unrest.

Over the next 10 years, millions of Americans eagerly read the muckrakers articles, which were published in many of the new popular national magazines. Ida Tarbell's series of articles on Standard Oil's business practices exposed many ills of American corporations, and Lincoln Steffens's investigations of scandal in city and state politics led to many political reforms. Upton Sinclair's exposure of abuses in the meatpacking industry helped lead to new health and safety standards. Other muckrakers' articles dealt with child labor, slum conditions, racial discrimination, and unfair manipulation of the stock market. In addition to the social reforms spurred by their articles, the muckrakers helped create the field of investigative journalism and strengthened the credibility and reputation of the professional press.

Ida Tarbell, one of the most prominent of the "muckrakers," is featured in this portrait. *(Library of Congress, Prints and Photographs Division [LC-USZ62-117943])*

ESTABLISHING "GOOD TASTE" AND OPPOSING "FIGHTING WORDS"

During the first half of the 1900s, the principles of free speech and free press were also challenged by new methods of communication, including motion pictures, radio, and television, as well as new and advanced modes of transportation that led to the growth of magazine and newspaper distribution. The person who most often dealt with these rapid changes was Anthony Comstock.

From the 1870s to the 1920s, Comstock was a special agent of the U.S. Post Office. For almost five decades, he worked, often successfully, to prevent the distribution of obscene material. In 1873, his influence led Congress to adopt the so-called Comstock Act, which read in part, "every obscene, lewd, or lascivious and every filthy books, painting, picture, paper, letter, writing or print . . . is a crime."

By the height of his influence in 1915, the term "Comstockery" was understood by supporters to mean any effort designed to protect

public morals and by detractors to mean unconstitutional restrictions on free expression. By the end of his career, Comstock, who
compared his job to standing at the mouth of a sewer, boasted that
he was responsible for the obscenity-related convictions of almost
3,000 people and the destruction of more than 50 tons of books and
close to 4 million pictures.

During the 1930s, concern about moral standards in speech
and print continued, even as court decisions permitted greater
expansion of free expression rights. In 1930, the Hays Code was
approved by the Motion Picture Producers and Distributors of
America (MPPDA), sometimes informally known as the Hays
Office. Led by Will Hays (the director of the MPDDA), this code
of ethics established standards of "good taste" for the booming
movie industry. Among the principles in the Hays Code were
requirements that "no picture shall be produced which will lower
the standards of those who see it. Hence the sympathy of the
audience should never be thrown to the side of crime, wrongdo-
ing, evil or sin." It also stated, "Pointed profanity (this includes
the words God, Lord, Jesus, Christ—unless used reverently—) . . .
or other profane or vulgar expressions, however used, is forbidden." Though violations of the Hays Code did not result in official prosecutions, these rules were rarely challenged by writers
and producers of the time.

Another example of unofficial censorship occurred in 1938,
when *Time* magazine published a series of photos taken from an
educational film entitled "The Birth of a Baby," detailing a woman's
life from the beginning to the end of a pregnancy. Some readers
were outraged by what they considered obscenely graphic photos,
and *Time* was pulled from the shelves in many cities around the
United States.

In 1942, the "clear and present danger" doctrine expressed by
the U.S. Supreme Court was expanded by its ruling in *Chaplinsky v.
New Hampshire*. In this case, the Court unanimously upheld the
conviction of Walter Chaplinsky, who was convicted under New
Hampshire's "fighting words" law after he distributed leaflets critical of all religion and cursing a city official. In its decision, the
Court explained,

> There are certain well-defined and narrowly limited classes of
> speech, the prevention and punishment of which have never been

thought to raise any constitutional problem. These include the lewd and obscene, the profane, the libelous, and the insulting or "fighting" words—those which by their very utterance inflict injury or tend to incite an immediate breach of the peace.

This case established an important precedent for laws and court cases on hate crimes that would come decades later.

FREE EXPRESSION DURING WORLD WAR II

The dominating event of the 1940s, World War II, also had a profound impact on the rights to free speech and press. Public opinion during the period of World War II (1941–45) was more supportive of individual rights to free expression than it was during the World

Preserving freedom of speech is displayed as a key reason for fighting in World War II, in this photo of a department store window display that shows the benefits of free expression and the danger of those who oppose it. *(Library of Congress, Prints and Photographs Division [LC-USZC2-131966])*

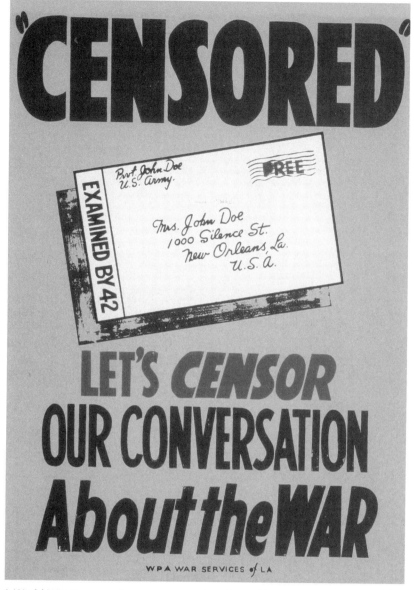

A World War II–era poster encourages American citizens to restrict their speech in order to ensure the security of U.S. troops. *(Library of Congress, Prints and Photographs Division [LC-USZC2-1588])*

War I era. Led by Justices William Douglas and Hugo Black, the U.S. Supreme Court ruled that criticism of government policy during wartime is not necessarily treason.

During World War II, fewer than 30 people served sentences for violations of the 1940 Smith Act, which made it a crime to teach or encourage "subversive" (intended to overthrow or undermine authority) ideas. Following Japan's attack on Pearl Harbor, which led to the U.S. entry into World War II, the occasional criticism of American war policy that did exist was largely tolerated and did not result in meaningful damage to the war effort.

In late summer 1945, Americans celebrated their victory in World War II and welcomed home thousands of soldiers who had bravely fought on the battlefields of Europe and Asia. Very quickly, however, new battlefields would form in the areas of free speech and the press at home.

5

Engaging Patriotism, Decency, and Race

In the memories and history books of most Americans, the 1950s and 1960s were very different. The 1950s are usually recalled as a time of calm social conformity and the 1960s are often remembered as a decade of turbulent domestic conflict. But both the 1950s and the 1960s were important eras of dynamic change, which would have an enormous impact on freedom of speech and the press, particularly as they related to the understanding of loyalty to the nation, the meaning of obscenity, and the advancement of civil rights.

THE McCARTHYISM ERA

As the 1950s began, the United States was again gripped by a red scare. This fear of communist influence was even more widespread and troubling than the one 30 years earlier. At this time, the United States was engaged in the early years of a cold war struggle with the Communist Soviet Union, fearful that their former World War II ally would continue to aggressively expand its belief in a single dominant political philosophy that opposed the basic political and economic principles of the United States. Nations such as Poland in Europe and China in Asia were now controlled by communist leaders, and millions in the United States worried that U.S. power and liberties were threatened. Into this fearful environment stepped a man who would occupy the center of the free speech and free press controversy—Senator Joseph McCarthy.

McCarthy was elected to the U.S. Senate by the people of Wisconsin in 1946. McCarthy's first few years in the Senate were unimpressive, and he began to worry that he might not get reelected. In 1950, McCarthy decided to try to boost his image and his reelection chances by seizing on American fears of communism. McCarthy blamed the recent U.S. setbacks in the cold war, including the Soviet Union's takeover of much of Eastern Europe and the communist revolution in China, on the disloyalty of American officials.

McCarthy gained attention and popularity by announcing that he had lists of known communists in the U.S. State Department. The number of names on his list often changed, and he rarely named those he claimed were on the list. When McCarthy named four people who had communist connections years earlier, his opponents accused him of unfair and ruthless smear tactics. He responded that their protests indicated that they were part of a larger communist conspiracy. Some of McCarthy's critics suffered politically, making McCarthy bolder in his assault on people's reputations and leading many of those disagreed with him to stay quiet.

The next few years would later become known as the era of McCarthyism. They were marked by McCarthy's personal witch hunt for communists in government and accusations and investigations of people's beliefs and actions, which were rarely backed up by solid evidence but which often ruined reputations and careers. McCarthy's slanderous attacks had a stunning effect on freedom of speech. In the early 1950s, the *Boston Post* pointed this out by explaining, "Attacking him in this state is regarded as a certain method of committing suicide."

McCarthy's targets were politicians and officials in the Democratic Party, artists, actors, and writers. Even the president of the United States, Dwight Eisenhower, was reluctant to challenge McCarthy publicly, despite disliking him and his methods intensely. Most journalists throughout the United States were slow to openly criticize McCarthy and his tactics, largely because of fear that doing so would lead them to be

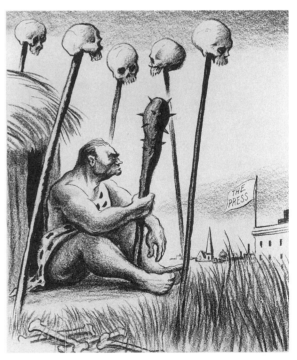

This cartoon criticizes the vicious tactics of Senator Joseph McCarthy and suggests that the press may be his next target. (*Reprinted with permission of the St. Louis Post-Dispatch, 2005*)

Edward R. Murrow, an early pioneer in radio and television journalism, is shown in this photo. *(Library of Congress, Prints and Photographs Division [LC-USZC2-126483])*

"We are not descended from fearful men—not from men who feared to write, to speak, to associate and to defend causes that were, for the moment, unpopular."

—*Edward R. Murrow, 1954*

labeled unpatriotic. Many of those who did openly condemn McCarthy or express political beliefs were often deemed traitors and occasionally blacklisted, tarnishing their reputations to the point that they were unable to gain employment.

In the beginning of 1954, McCarthy's firm grip on free expression in the United States began to loosen, largely because of the influence of newspaper writers and reporters from the new popular communication medium—television. In March 1954, CBS News broadcaster Edward Murrow used his television news show *See It Now* to examine the bullying nature of McCarthyism and its chilling effect on freedom of expression. After documenting cases of McCarthy's abuse, Murrow concluded the program by saying, "We must not confuse dissent with disloyalty. We must remember always that accusation is not proof and that conviction depends upon evidence and due process of law."

A few months after this broadcast, McCarthy conducted an investigation of communist influence in the U.S. Army. American viewers were riveted to their television sets throughout the month-and-a-half duration of the Army-McCarthy hearings. The live coverage exposed McCarthy's irresponsible use of power. When McCarthy again lobbed an unfounded accusation of communism at an army officer, army lawyer Joseph Welch famously shot back, "Until this moment, Senator, I think I never gauged your cruelty or your recklessness . . . Have you no sense of decency, sir?" Later in the proceedings, Senator Stuart Symington sharply explained to McCarthy, "The American people have had a look at you for six weeks. You are not fooling anyone."

Leading politicians in both parties began openly condemning McCarthy. In December 1954, he was *censured* (officially charged with severe disapproval) for his actions, though he remained in the Senate. Less than two and a half years later, McCarthy died of an illness related to excessive alcohol abuse.

In the decades since the height of his influence, Joseph McCarthy has remained a symbol of how the irresponsible use of freedom of speech by an influential person can stifle the freedom of speech of others. The era of McCarthyism is also remembered as a fearful time brought to an end largely because of the press's ability to freely report and examine the conduct of elected leaders.

SEEKING A DEFINITION OF OBSCENITY

The 1950s also featured the Supreme Court's first major review of the controversial free expression issue of obscenity. Laws against the sale, display, and possession of obscene material first appeared in the United States at the beginning of the 1800s. At that time, the idea that obscenity might be difficult to define was not given a great deal of attention by the American people or the courts. For the next century and a half, the Supreme Court rarely considered whether restrictions of obscenity were constitutional, and when it did, it always found such material outside the protection of the First Amendment. During this time, even material that seemed to have artistic or literary value was restricted if it contained images or words considered obscene.

But for a growing number of Americans, this seemingly *arbitrary* (random, varying by individual) definition of obscenity led to the question: What is obscenity? What one person considers racy and harmless might be thought of by someone else as filthy and morally dangerous. As attitudes and technology changed, leading to increased production and purchasing of material deemed obscene, the need for clarification of this issue grew. The Supreme Court attempted to provide this guidance in the 1957 case of *Roth v. United States.*

Samuel Roth was a New York businessman who published and sold books and magazines containing pictures of naked women. He was charged and convicted of violating federal obscenity laws when he mailed material advertising his publications. Roth challenged his conviction, claiming that it violated the First Amendment's guarantee protecting freedom of speech and the press.

In a 5-4 decision, the Supreme Court upheld Roth's conviction, but the decision did not by any means settle the issues of defining obscenity or to what extent the government should be able to restrict it. In the majority opinion, Justice William Brennan wrote:

> "One man's vulgarity is another's lyric."
>
> —*Supreme Court Justice John Harlan, 1971*

Implicit in the history of the First Amendment is the rejection of obscenity as utterly without redeeming social importance. . . . We hold that obscenity is not within the area of constitutionally protected speech or press . . . However, sex and obscenity are not synonymous. Obscene material is material which deals with sex in a manner appealing to prurient [lustful] interest . . . It is therefore vital that the standards for judging obscenity safeguard the protection of freedom of speech and press for material which does not treat sex in a manner appealing to prurient interest.

Brennan offered the "community standards" test to evaluate whether material was obscene, asking "whether to the average person, applying contemporary community standards, the dominant theme of the material taken as a whole appeals to prurient interest."

In Justice William O. Douglas's dissenting opinion, he described the problems with this new judicial attempt to define obscenity, writing, "Any test that turns of what is offensive to the community's standards is too loose . . . too destructive of freedom of expression to be squared with the First Amendment. Under that test, juries can censor, suppress, or punish what they don't like, provided the matter relates to sexual impurity or has a tendency to excite lustful thoughts. This is community censorship in one of its worst forms."

The *subjective* (based on an individual's standards) nature of deciding what is obscene continued to cause controversy throughout the 1960s and into the 1970s.

THE WARREN COURT

Earl Warren was governor of California when President Dwight Eisenhower chose him to serve as the new chief justice of the Supreme Court in 1953. For the next 16 years, Warren led the Court through some of its most controversial cases dealing with the freedoms of speech and the press, such as 1957's *Roth v. United States* and 1964's *New York Times v. Sullivan*.

In those cases and many others during this time, Warren helped lead a more active role for the Supreme Court, taking on the defense of individual rights as no court before it. Warren did not see the role of the judiciary as passive or inferior to the other two branches of government, and he believed that the Constitution prohibited the government from acting unfairly against the individual.

In 1974, the Supreme Court again tried to further clarify the issue in *Jenkins v. Georgia.* In this case, a Georgia jury convicted a movie theater operator for showing the popular R-rated film *Carnal Knowledge.* The small-town jury believed that the film appealed to "prurient interests" and was "patently offensive" to community standards. However, unlike the material reviewed in other obscenity-related cases, *Carnal Knowledge* was a critically acclaimed film and it had been shown in dozens of other Georgia towns without incident or complaint.

The Supreme Court overturned the conviction of the theater owner, explaining "our own viewing . . . satisfies us that 'Carnal Knowledge' could not be found . . . to depict sexual conduct in a patently offensive way." Though this decision was celebrated by most advocates of First Amendment rights, it provided even more evidence of how blurry the definition of obscenity remained.

Two other high-profile Supreme Court cases from the 1970s and 1980s sought to clarify the complex meaning of obscenity. In 1978, a radio station in New York City, WBAI-FM, aired a 12-minute routine from a popular 1972 album by comedian George Carlin. The routine, which was broadcast at 2:00 P.M., focused on the "seven dirty words" that were not allowed to be said on radio or television. The Federal Communications Commission (FCC), established by the U.S. government in 1934 to provide regulation of the airwaves, responded to complaints about the broadcast of Carlin's routine and sought to punish the company that owned the radio station. The station's ownership argued that the routine was protected by the First Amendment guarantee of free speech.

But the Supreme Court disagreed. In a 5-4 decision in *Federal Communications Commission v. Pacifica Foundation,* the Court ruled that the FCC was permitted to sanction broadcasters for obscene, indecent, or profane language, particularly if the material is broadcasted during a time when children are likely to be in the audience. The FCC still can punish station owners for violations of standards, though material that might be considered indecent has usually been allowed during "safe harbor" hours of 10:00 P.M. to 6:00 A.M.

Another famous freedom-of-the-press indecency case took place in 1984. In *Hustler v. Falwell,* religious and political activist Reverend Jerry Falwell sued pornography publisher Larry Flynt and his *Hustler Magazine* for a satirical (fake; designed to amuse)

"There are over 400,000 words in the English language and there are seven of them that you can't say on television . . . They must really be bad."

—*George Carlin, 1972*

advertisement that ridiculed the reverend and his mother with obscene imagery. Flynt admitted that the ad was insulting and in bad taste, but contended that because the ad clearly noted "Ad parody—not to be taken seriously," he should not be found guilty of libel. Flynt also felt that Falwell should not be entitled to the $200,000 award for "emotional distress" given to him by a jury. The Supreme Court unanimously ruled in favor of Flynt, explaining that bad taste is not against the law and that satire directed at public figures is a form of expression protected by the First Amendment.

FREE SPEECH AND PRESS SPURS THE CIVIL RIGHTS MOVEMENT

The 1950s and 1960s were also witness to critical developments in freedom of speech and the press that had a powerful impact on the Civil Rights movement. Between 1954 and 1956, three major events occurred that galvanized the drive to end racial segregation in the South: the unanimous Supreme Court decision in *Brown v. Board of Education* prohibiting segregation in public schools; the murder of a black teenager from Chicago, Emmett Till, by whites in Mississippi; and the refusal of black passenger Rosa Parks to observe custom and sit in the back of a Montgomery, Alabama, bus. All three were important events publicized by the news media, especially the emerging field of television news.

The popularity of television leaped in the 1950s and so did the growth of television journalism. News programmers needed to fill their expanded coverage with important and compelling stories. Their freedom to vividly portray the dramatic events taking place in the Civil Rights movement helped swell the ranks of civil rights organizations and educated millions of whites who previously did not know or did not care to know the effects of racial segregation. This press coverage also led to a backlash among many southerners who resented the presence and influence of "outsiders."

This conflict played out in the courts in the early 1960s, culminating in the 1964 Supreme Court case *New York Times v. Sullivan*. On March 29, 1960, the *New York Times* carried an advertisement from a group of southern clergymen and others soliciting funds for civil rights organizations. The ad included a few minor inaccuracies

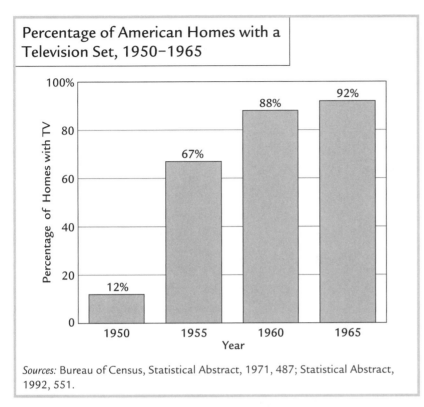

Percentage of American Homes with a Television Set, 1950–1965

Sources: Bureau of Census, Statistical Abstract, 1971, 487; Statistical Abstract, 1992, 551.

The rapid growth of television ownership in the United States greatly influenced how Americans saw, experienced, and interpreted news events.

and featured complaints about a variety of actions against young civil rights workers and the movement's charismatic leader Dr. Martin Luther King, Jr., by officials in Montgomery, Alabama, though it did not mention anyone by name. Montgomery Police Chief L. B. Sullivan sued the paper for libel for carrying the ad, arguing that "everyone knew" who was being criticized in the piece. An Alabama jury awarded a $500,000 settlement to Sullivan even though no clear damages to his reputation had been proven.

The Supreme Court unanimously overruled the judgment of the Alabama court, striking a strong blow for the free reporting of civil rights activities in the South. The ruling established a standard of actual malice, requiring that a publisher must know that a statement is false or acts in reckless disregard of the truth in order to be punished.

President John Kennedy helped elevate the right to a free press and the power of television journalism by increasing the number of presidential press conferences, such as the one pictured here from 1962, where he met with reporters to discuss important issues. *(Abbie Rowe, National Park Service/ John Fitzgerald Kennedy Library, Boston)*

Before this decision there was nearly $300 million in libel lawsuits against news organizations relating to coverage of the Civil Rights movement. This caused many publications to avoid reporting certain stories because of fear of legal action. The *New York Times* and other publications claimed that these lawsuits and threats were intended to intimidate them and prevent the open reporting of illegal actions of southern officials who supported segregation. After the *Sullivan* decision, fear among the press decreased and freedom to report the news accurately increased.

ETHEL PAYNE
First Lady of the Black Press

Ethel Payne was working as a hostess for the U.S. Army in Tokyo in the late 1940s when she shared her journal with a visiting reporter from the *Chicago Defender*, a leading African-American newspaper with a national following. The reporter was impressed with Payne's writing style and her insight about her own experiences and those of black soldiers. Her stories soon were featured in the *Defender*, and a few years later she moved to Chicago to work full time for the newspaper.

During Payne's career, she earned a reputation as a sharp journalist who asked tough questions. She covered several key events in the Civil Rights movement, including the Montgomery bus boycott, the desegregation of the University of Alabama in 1956, and the 1963 March on Washington. In 1972 she became the first female African-American commentator employed by a national network, when she was hired as a commentator by CBS.

THE IMPACT OF MARTIN LUTHER KING, JR.

Coverage of the Civil Rights movement became even more prominent during the mid to late 1960s, and it often focused on the speeches of leaders, chief among them Martin Luther King, Jr. His August 29, 1963, address to more than 300,000 people on the Washington, D.C., Mall and millions watching on television and listening to their radios reflected the impact of free speech. As with Frederick Douglass more than 100 years earlier, King's words both powered a movement and remain solidly fixed in American memory:

> I have a dream that one day this nation will rise up and live out the true meaning of its creed. "We hold these truths to be self-evident: that all men are created equal.". . . I have a dream that my four children will one day live in a nation where they will not be judged by the color of their skin but by the content of their character.

Tragically, King would be murdered less than five years later, at age 38. The evening before he was killed, King strengthened the legacy of free expression with words that resounded with the American hope that the nation will meet its promise of equality and

> "Our lives begin to end the day we become silent about things that matter."
>
> —*Martin Luther King, Jr., (1929–1968)*

The Reverend Martin Luther King, Jr., waves to a huge crowd before he delivers his "I Have a Dream" speech at the 1963 March on Washington. *(UPI/Landov)*

opportunity: "We've got some difficult days ahead . . . Like anybody I would like to live a long life. Longevity has its place . . . But I want you to know tonight, that we, as a people, will get to the promised land!"

6

Vietnam and Watergate

Alongside the Civil Rights movement, two other events dominated the headlines during the 10-year period between 1964 and 1974. Each of these events, the Vietnam War and the Watergate scandal, divided the nation and had a powerful impact on the developing influence of the freedoms of speech and the press.

On August 5, 1964, newspapers across the United States ran stories describing a confrontation the previous evening between U.S. warships and North Vietnamese PT boats in the Gulf of Tonkin, just off the coast of Vietnam. Although it is still not entirely clear how the skirmish on that dark and rainy night began, articles at the time conveyed the viewpoint of President Lyndon Johnson's administration that the fighting was caused by an unprovoked attack on peaceful U.S. patrols. President Johnson, flush with the overwhelming support of the American people and Congress, quickly gained passage of the Gulf of Tonkin Resolution, which provided him the power to "take all necessary steps, including the use of armed forces" to repel attack and support allies in Southeast Asia. This marked the beginning of the U.S. combat role in Vietnam and led to an era of important new developments for the First Amendment freedoms of speech and the press.

SYMBOLIC SPEECH

During the first few years of fighting, most Americans supported the U.S. role in Vietnam. However, there were many who objected to the war. Among this group were three students in Des Moines,

Iowa: 16-year-old Christopher Eckhardt, 15-year-old John Tinker, and his sister 13-year-old Mary Beth Tinker.

In December 1965, these three teenagers wore black armbands to school to express their opposition to the Vietnam War. This form of symbolic speech violated the Des Moines School District's policy forbidding the wearing of armbands to school, a policy that had been passed after rumors of the students' intentions began to spread. After Eckhardt and the older Tinker wore the armbands to their high school and the younger Tinker wore them to her junior high school, all of them were suspended. Their families then sued the school board, resulting in the Supreme Court case *Tinker et. al. v. Des Moines Independent School District.*

Lower courts found in favor of the school board's decision to suspend the students. In the Supreme Court case, lawyers for the school board argued that the wearing of the armbands was intended to disrupt school activities and in fact did so. When evidence was revealed that there was little or no significant disruption in the learning environment caused by the wearing of the armbands, the school board lawyers claimed it was because of the school board's swift action in suspending the students. The school board lawyers had a more difficult time explaining why the armbands were banned while other forms of political expression, such as campaign buttons, had traditionally been allowed.

The lawyers for the Tinker and Eckhardt families claimed that the wearing of the armbands was a peaceful form of political protest that was protected by the First Amendment and not disruptive of the school's learning environment. Ultimately, their cause was supported by a 7-2 majority of Supreme Court justices. Writing for the majority, Justice Abe Fortas explained, "First Amendment rights, applied in light of the special characteristics of the school environment, are available to teachers and students. It can hardly be argued that either students or teachers shed their constitutional rights to freedom of speech or expression at the schoolhouse gate . . ."

Justice Hugo Black, who had been a longtime advocate for free expression, disagreed, writing in his dissenting opinion, "While I have always believed that under the First and Fourteenth Amendments neither the state nor the federal government has any authority to regulate or censor the content of speech, I have never believed that any person has a right to give speeches or engage in demonstrations where he pleases and when he pleases . . ."

Fortas countered this argument, reasoning ". . . school authorities did not . . . prohibit the wearing of all symbols of political or controversial significance . . . Instead a particular symbol—black armbands worn to exhibit opposition to this nation's involvement in Vietnam—was singled out for prohibition. Clearly, the prohibition of expression of one particular opinion, at least without evidence that it is necessary to avoid . . . substantial interference with schoolwork or discipline, is not constitutionally permissible."

The Tinker decision was just one indication of the controversy within the United States regarding the Vietnam War, though it did strike a blow for students' rights in that school boards maintained wide control over the free expression of students. Speech, even symbolic speech such as the kind expressed by the students involved in the Tinker case, can be restricted if it can be persuasively argued that it will significantly disrupt the learning process. So although, as Fortas explained, students do not "shed their constitutional rights at the schoolhouse gate," they do not always possess these rights to the same degree they might outside the school.

> "In a democracy, dissent is an act of faith. Like medicine, the test of its value is not in its taste, but its effects."
>
> —Senator William Fulbright, 1966

NEWS MEDIA COVERAGE OF THE VIETNAM WAR

The Vietnam War's relationship to First Amendment rights was also widely seen in the growing influence and power of the press. As the war in Vietnam dragged on and the expectations held by many Americans for a quick and decisive victory were not realized, many in the press became more skeptical of the steady stream of optimistic reports from U.S. military and political leaders, including President Lyndon Johnson who promised a "light at the end of the tunnel" and "victory just around the corner." By 1968, when the U.S. troop commitment swelled to more than 500,000, newspaper reporters and television correspondents increasingly portrayed the war as a stalemate, directly and indirectly questioning the wisdom of continued fighting. These opinions contributed greatly to the breakdown of the previously solid support among Americans for the U.S. role in the Vietnam War.

This influence was most noticeable in television journalism. Largely because of advancements in electronic and satellite technol-

> "Hey, hey, LBJ, how many kids did you kill today?!"
>
> —Anti-Vietnam War protest chant, 1960s

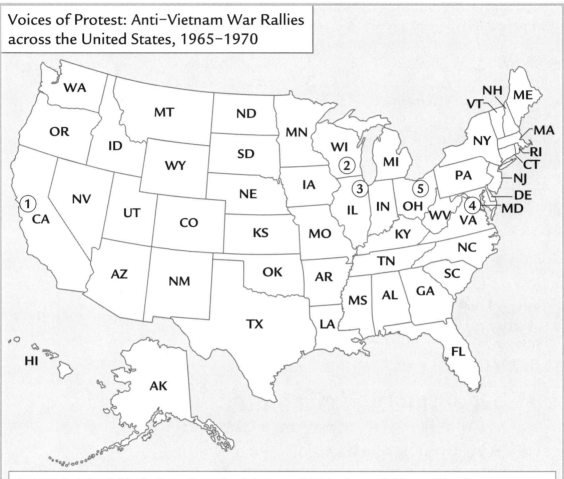

Voices of Protest: Anti-Vietnam War Rallies across the United States, 1965–1970

1. **1965, Berkeley, California:** First major student-led protest of U.S. involvement in Vietnam War takes place on campus of University of California.
2. **1967, Madison Wisconsin:** Protesters at the University of Wisconsin speak out against recruitment of students by company that provided chemicals used by U.S. military in Vietnam.
3. **1968, Chicago, Illinois:** Antiwar demonstrators clash with police outside of Democratic National Convention.
4. **1969, Washington, D.C.:** Vietnam Moratorium marches occur across United States; 500,000 march in nations's capital alone.
5. **1970, Kent State University, Ohio:** Ohio National Guard fires on antiwar protesters, killing four.

ogy, the Vietnam War became known as "The Living Room War," reflecting the way that the frustrations and horrors of combat were broadcast more immediately and vividly into American homes than ever before. The power and freedom of television journalists was most clearly demonstrated on the night of February 27, 1968, when

CBS Evening News anchor Walter Cronkite, widely considered the most trusted man in America, delivered a rare editorial following a special broadcast on the Vietnam War. Noting his recent visit to Vietnam, Cronkite said:

> *To say that we are closer to victory today is to believe, in the face of the evidence, the optimists who have been wrong in the past. To suggest we are on the edge of defeat is to yield to unreasonable pessimism. To say that we are mired in stalemate seems the only realistic, yet unsatisfactory, conclusion . . . But it is increasingly clear to this reporter that the only rational way out then will be to negotiate, not as victors, but as an honorable people who lived up to their pledge to defend democracy, and did the best they could.*

Watching this from the White House, President Johnson turned off the television and somberly stated, "If I've lost Cronkite, I've lost Middle America." Less than five weeks later, Johnson surprised the nation by announcing that he would not seek another term as president in the 1968 election.

President Lyndon Johnson is shown announcing that he will not run for reelection in 1968 following increased vocal protest and press criticism over his handling of the Vietnam War. *(Lyndon Baines Johnson Library and Museum)*

ANTIWAR PROTESTERS' EFFECTS ON PRESIDENT JOHNSON

By early spring 1968, President Lyndon Johnson had clearly heard the voices of antiwar protesters. He would later recall: "Every night when I fell asleep, I would see myself tied to the ground in the middle of a long open space. In the distance, I could hear the voices of thousands of people. They were all shouting at me and running towards me: 'Coward, traitor, weakling!' They kept coming closer. They began throwing stones. At exactly that moment, I would wake up."

On March 31, 1968, looking much older than his 59 years, Johnson addressed the nation in a televised speech. He shocked the nation with the announcement that he would not seek another term as president. He died fewer than five years later—less than a week before the United States ended its combat role in the Vietnam War.

THE PENTAGON PAPERS

The press also underwent major changes during and because of the Vietnam War. One example of this is the 1971 Supreme Court case of *New York Times v. United States,* better known as the Pentagon Papers case.

The Pentagon Papers were a top-secret U.S. government study tracing U.S. involvement in Southeast Asia, specifically Vietnam, from World War II to May 1968. It was ordered by Secretary of Defense Robert McNamara in June 1967 and was written for more than a year and a half by a team of analysts who had access to classified documents. The study showed that U.S. presidents and high-ranking civilian and military leaders had miscalculated the risks and conditions of military involvement in Vietnam and misled the American people about the U.S. role throughout the region.

Excerpts from the study were secretly given to the *New York Times* by Daniel Ellsberg, who was one of the analysts involved in the research. On June 13, 1971, the *Times* began publishing a series of articles based on the documents, which became known as the Pentagon Papers. After the *Times* printed its third installment of the Pentagon Papers, the Justice Department of President Richard Nixon's administration asked for and received a restraining order to prevent the newspapers from publishing material based on the study. If the *Times* published the remaining articles in its series, the government argued, it would bring "immediate and irreparable harm" to the "national defense interests of the United States and the nation's security."

This constitutional conflict quickly was reviewed by the Supreme Court in the case of *New York Times v. United States*. In this case, the government claimed that it should be the sole judge of national security needs and should be allowed to prevent further publication of the Pentagon Papers. The *Times* countered that this would violate press freedoms provided by the First Amendment. It also argued that the real government motive was political censorship rather than protection of national security, explaining that much of the information contained in the Pentagon Papers had already been revealed by government officials themselves.

On June 30, 1971, the Supreme Court ruled 6-3 in favor of the *New York Times*, and the documents were quickly published. In allowing the newspaper to continue the series the Court noted that the Constitution has a "heavy presumption" in favor of press freedom. The Court left open the possibility that dire consequences could result from publication of classified documents by newspapers, but it said that the government had failed to prove that result in this instance.

The legacy of the Pentagon Papers continued to evolve following the Supreme Court's decision to allow their publication. Frustration and anger over the U.S. role in the Vietnam War among Americans increased, even as the United States reduced its troop commitment. In 1971, Daniel Ellsberg was indicted for theft, espionage, and conspiracy for his role in bringing the classified information to the newspaper. Charges against Ellsberg were dismissed in 1973 after it was discovered that the government had acted improperly during its prosecution of him. Perhaps the most enduring effect of the Pentagon Papers can be understood in the words of Supreme Court Justice Hugo Black, who wrote in the case's majority opinion: "Only a free and unrestrained press can effectively expose deception in government."

TENSION BETWEEN THE PRESS AND AMERICAN MILITARY LEADERS

The widespread protests of the Vietnam War and the Pentagon Papers case showed how First Amendment protections of free speech and free press had been strengthened. But soon there was a backlash, as many American political and military leaders were embarrassed by the extent of the protests and believed that the attention given to them by the press hurt the war effort.

The most famous case of antiwar protest may have been the demonstrations outside the 1968 Democratic National Convention in Chicago. These protests led to violent clashes between the demonstrators and Chicago police. Amidst the chaos, protesters showed their awareness of the power and reach of the free press by chanting "The whole world is watching!"

This incident, and others like it, further divided the American people between those who were angered about what they saw as the crackdown on the exercise of free speech and those who viewed this speech as irresponsible and even treasonous. In 1969, President Richard Nixon reflected the views of these people when he appealed to "the great silent majority" of Americans to continue support of the U.S. effort in Vietnam.

Photographers, such as Terry Fincher and Larry Burrows, pictured here during the Vietnam War, have played a critical role in bringing the stories of battles to readers. *(Express Newspapers/Getty Images)*

Many in the U.S. military also viewed the Vietnam War–era influence of free speech and free press with concern. During the Vietnam War, reporters had only two basic restrictions: They were not allowed to report troop movements prior to battle, and they were prohibited from showing the faces of dead or wounded American soldiers until their families had been properly identified and notified. Although there were virtually no violations of these guidelines by U.S. news organizations, there was a common belief among the military that this open policy helped shift public opinion against the war, with some feeling that the press lost the Vietnam War for the United States.

Press coverage has been more restricted in U.S. military encounters since the Vietnam War. During the U.S. military operations in the Caribbean island of Grenada in 1983, in Panama in 1989, during the Persian Gulf War in 1990–91, and in the Iraq War that began in 2003, prohibitions on the press were far tighter than during the Vietnam War. Examples of these access restrictions have included cases of military selection of correspondents who serve in pools of reporters and security reviews of stories by news organizations before their release. The tension between the desire to inform the public and express dissent while not endangering the lives of soldiers continues to be at the center of one of the most important and fiercely debated First Amendment controversies.

> "Vietnam was the first war ever fought without any censorship. Without censorship, things can get terribly confused in the public mind."
>
> —*General William Westmoreland, 1982*

UNCOVERING WATERGATE

As the United States was emerging from the turbulent years of the Vietnam War, a new scandal came to dominate the headlines and powerfully affect the First Amendment rights of freedom of speech and freedom of the press. It was known as Watergate.

On June 17, 1972, five men were arrested after breaking into the headquarters of the Democratic National Committee in Washington, D.C.'s, Watergate Hotel. At first the story did not receive much attention in the press. But when one of the men was linked to the Committee to Re-elect the President, it soon became a major focus of interest despite the description of the event by President Nixon's press secretary as a "third-rate burglary."

Two young reporters from the *Washington Post,* Bob Woodward and Carl Bernstein, began an investigation of the Watergate break-in. Much of what they published kept the growing scandal

The *Washington Post* reporters who broke the Watergate story, Carl Bernstein (left) and Bob Woodward (right), are pictured here talking to their publisher, Katharine Graham, in 1973. *(© Mark Godfrey/ The Image Works)*

in the spotlight and embarrassed President Nixon and many of his aides, who maintained that they had no involvement.

With the help of an anonymous source code-named "Deep Throat" (who revealed himself in 2005 as former high-ranking FBI official W. Mark Felt), Woodward and Bernstein continued to uncover details in the Watergate story that shocked the nation. From their reporting, and the testimony of some of the people who were involved in the break-in, a string of misdeeds and cover-ups were exposed, committed by or in the name of President Nixon. Among Woodward and Bernstein's discoveries was the use of "dirty tricks" undertaken on behalf of President Nixon to undermine his opponents, including antiwar protesters such as Daniel Ellsberg, who had leaked the Pentagon Papers to the *New York Times*.

"The press is the enemy."

President Richard Nixon in a private remark to aides, 1969

THE EFFECTS OF WATERGATE

Following Woodward and Bernstein's lead, other news organizations joined the investigation of Watergate, resulting in more revelations, the resignation of top Nixon aides, the formation of an independent legal team to investigate the growing scandal, and special hearings in the U.S. Senate. The hearings of the Senate Watergate Committee began in May 1973 and were televised live throughout the United States. During the course of these hearings, more scandalous details were uncovered, including testimony that President Nixon had secretly recorded all of his conversations held in the Oval Office of the White House. When legal requests were made for President Nixon to hand over these tapes, he refused, citing the executive privilege of his job and the need to protect national security.

Things continued to unravel for President Nixon. With the heat of press coverage fueling anger and suspicion of him and his administration, President Nixon relented and allowed portions of the tapes to be heard. The Senate and the independent legal team, however, wanted access to all of them, leading to the 1974 Supreme Court case *United States v. Nixon*. In this case, the Supreme Court ruled unanimously against the president, ordering him to surrender the tapes. One of the newly released tapes was the "smoking gun"—proof that President Nixon knew of the Watergate break-in and actively participated in its cover-up.

Within a few weeks, it became obvious that President Nixon did not have the support of the people or his former supporters in

RICHARD NIXON'S TENSE RELATIONSHIP WITH THE PRESS

Throughout Richard Nixon's long political career, he consistently distrusted the press. In 1952, he appeared on national television in his famous "Checkers Speech" to refute charges made in the press that he misused funds as a senator. Nixon explained that the only gift he had received as a politician was a dog named Checkers and that he would not be returning him because his young daughters loved the animal so much.

After eight years as vice president, Nixon ran for governor of California in 1962. When he lost that election, he criticized the press, telling them at a press conference, "Just think of how much you'll be missing. You won't have Nixon to kick around anymore." His secretly recorded conversations as president, exposed by the Watergate scandal, also reflect his obsession with press coverage. Among the recordings is an excerpt from April 27, 1973, in which Nixon said of the press, ". . . they're cannibals . . . They hate my guts."

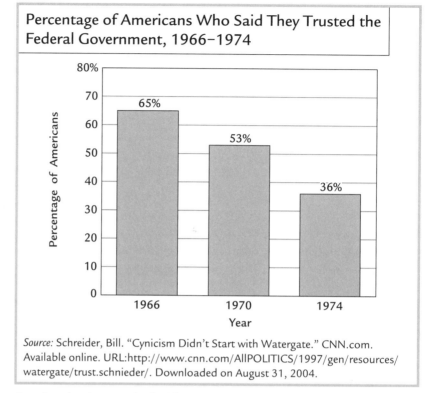

Percentage of Americans Who Said They Trusted the Federal Government, 1966–1974

Source: Schreider, Bill. "Cynicism Didn't Start with Watergate." CNN.com. Available online. URL:http://www.cnn.com/AllPOLITICS/1997/gen/resources/watergate/trust.schnieder/. Downloaded on August 31, 2004.

American involvement in the Vietnam War (1964–73) and the Watergate scandal (1972–74) had an enormous impact on the public's trust in the federal government.

the U.S. Congress. Faced with near certain impeachment, President Nixon became the only president to resign his office, on August 9, 1974.

The effects of the Watergate scandal did not end with the resignation of the president. In a significant way, Watergate was the spark that led to new laws and the strengthening of old laws intended to prevent abuse of governmental power. Included among these was the expansion of the Freedom of Information Act (FOIA). Though originally passed in 1968, the FOIA was changed immediately after Watergate to provide any person the right of access to federal agency records or information. The FOIA puts the burden on the government to explain why information should not be released. Upon formal written request,

ALL THE PRESIDENT'S MEN

In 1976, *Washington Post* reporters Bob Woodward and Carl Bernstein wrote *All the President's Men*, a book about their experience investigating and exposing the details of Watergate. The book quickly became the number-one best-seller in the nation. Later that year, a movie of the same title was released and it also was immediately enormously popular, eventually receiving several Academy Award nominations.

Both the book and the movie contributed to a boom in the popularity of investigative journalism, as reporters gained influence, status, fame, and even fortune by uncovering and exposing scandalous stories. Although the growth of investigative journalism is often credited with demonstrating how the press serves as the primary watchdog of government officials, it has also led to concerns over the role of gossip, controversy, sensationalism, and manufactured scandal that have led many to be more cynical about the press, politics, and public policy.

agencies of the U.S. government are required to disclose those records unless they can be lawfully withheld under one of the nine exemptions, including endangering national security, that are part of the law.

Watergate broadened the scope of the free press in the United States in other ways. Since Watergate, the mass media has become far more aggressive in reporting on the background and activities of politicians' personal lives. Financial disclosures, including the release of income tax information, are now expected, though not required, of major political candidates. In addition, incidents that the press would have been very unlikely to mention before Watergate, such as alcohol abuse or marital infidelity, are often reported and have led to the end of political careers.

The free-expression legacy of the Vietnam War and the Watergate scandal is remembered every time someone voices concern that a military action will lead to "another Vietnam" or adds the suffix "-gate" to the end of a term associated with scandal. These events had a powerful impact on perception and reality of the First Amendment rights to free speech and free press in the United States and continued to have a strong influence as the nation approached a new century.

7

Battles over Hateful Words

The rights to free expression were both strained and strengthened by the Vietnam War and Watergate. They would soon be severely tested again in a classic conflict over whether the bigoted and widely rejected beliefs of a small group of people were protected by the First Amendment.

NEO-NAZIS PLAN A MARCH IN SKOKIE, ILLINOIS

In spring 1977 a neo-Nazi organization decided to hold a demonstration in the village of Skokie, Illinois, just north of Chicago. Outrage over the neo-Nazis' presence in the town among its large Jewish population as well as its non-Jewish residents led to concerns over what might happen if they were allowed to demonstrate. Because of these concerns, Skokie's political leaders sought and obtained an injunction preventing the march.

Because of the First Amendment issues involved in this case, the Illinois affiliate of the ACLU agreed to defend the free speech rights of the neo-Nazis. As a result of the ACLU's work on behalf of the neo-Nazis, almost 20 percent of the ACLU's approximately 250,000 members left the organization in protest. The ACLU's executive director, Aryeh Neier, a Jew who lost relatives in the Holocaust, understood the anger of those who quit but explained, "Keeping a few Nazis off the streets of Skokie will serve Jews poorly if it means that the freedoms to speak, publish, or assemble any place in the United States are thereby weakened."

After a series of court battles, the Illinois Appellate Court ruled in July 1977 that the neo-Nazis could march in Skokie, but they were forbidden to display or wear the swastika because doing so would represent the kind of "fighting words" not protected by the First Amendment since the *Chaplinsky v. New Hampshire* decision in 1942. The ACLU fought this as well, arguing that the swastika should be a fully protected form of symbolic speech, just as black armbands worn to protest the Vietnam War were. The ACLU also countered arguments made by many of Skokie's leaders that they would not be able to control the intense reaction by residents against the neo-Nazis if they were allowed to demonstrate by explaining that it is unconstitutional to ban speech on the basis of a "heckler's veto."

The debate over the neo-Nazis' proposed demonstration in Skokie raged across the United States, with most people believing that there should be some limits to free speech and that the public speech of the neo-Nazis, particularly in a largely Jewish area, was beyond those limits. More than 500,000 Americans signed petitions supporting Skokie's efforts to prevent the neo-Nazi rally. Journalists weighed in on the issue as well. An editorial in the magazine *The Nation* supported the neo-Nazis' rights despite disagreeing with their views by noting that if town authorities had been allowed to prohibit demonstrations based on fears that they would endanger the peace, then many of the historic civil rights marches of the 1960s would never have occurred.

This reasoning did little to change the views of those who felt the neo-Nazis had no right to march in Skokie. The thoughts of many of these people were captured by a *New York Post* reader who wrote to the newspaper, "It's very simple really: Those

This 1973 photo of a neo-Nazi rally in Washington, D.C., shows how the U.S. government protects freedom of speech even for ideas that most people completely reject. *(Hulton Archive/Getty Images)*

WHY THE NEO-NAZIS CHOSE SKOKIE

When Adolf Hitler came to power in Germany in 1933, one of his first acts of power was to stifle free speech and the free press rights of German citizens. In this atmosphere of repression and fear, he then set about planning and carrying out the genocide of Jewish people throughout Germany and later the parts of Europe that Germany had taken over during World War II.

When World War II ended in 1945, Hitler had committed suicide, but more than 6 million Jews had been murdered by his regime of terror. Many of the Jewish survivors of what became known as the Holocaust settled in the United States. They vowed that never again would such a tragedy happen to them. The group of American neo-Nazis that applied for and eventually received permission to rally in Skokie chose the town because more than half of the town's 60,000 residents were Jewish, and more than 5,000 were survivors of the Nazi Holocaust of European Jews during World War II.

---

who (by word or deed) seek to undermine and destroy the basic tenets of the Constitution, at the time relinquish its protection for themselves." For them, the Constitution was not a suicide pact that should allow those who do not believe in free expression to use its freedoms to oppress others and ultimately destroy the liberties of the document itself.

However, legal challenges to the neo-Nazis' wish to demonstrate continued to fail, including a Skokie ordinance that required the neo-Nazis to come up with a $350,000 high-liability insurance policy to cover possible damage caused by the rally. Rejecting one of the legal challenges brought by Skokie, a federal appeals court explained that it would be "grossly insensitive to deny . . . that the proposed demonstration would seriously disturb, emotionally and mentally, at least some, and probably many of the village's residents," and added that if First Amendment rights "are to remain vital for all, they must protect not only those society deems acceptable, but also those whose ideas it quite justifiably rejects and despises."

Finally, Skokie appealed to the U.S. Supreme Court to hear the case, but it refused, clearing the way for the neo-Nazis' rally to proceed. A few days before their scheduled march, the neo-Nazis decided to hold a demonstration in Chicago instead. Counterdemonstrators vastly outnumbered the neo-Nazis, and police maintained order.

> "The ability of American society to tolerate the advocacy of even hateful doctrines . . . is perhaps the best protection we have against the establishment of any Nazi-type regime."
>
> —*Judge Bernard Decker, 1978*

SPEECH CODES ON COLLEGE CAMPUSES

In the 1980s and early 1990s, battles over the First Amendment rights to free speech and free press increasingly focused on hate speech. Some of the most publicized and controversial of these battles were fought on college campuses across the United States, which have enacted speech codes designed to combat discrimination and harassment.

The speech code at the University of Michigan, passed in 1988, reflected the guidelines included in many other campus speech codes. The policy prohibited "[a]ny behavior, verbal or physical, that stigmatizes or victimizes an individual on the basis of race, ethnicity, religion, sex, sexual orientation, creed . . . and that . . . creates an intimidating, hostile, or demeaning environment for educational pursuits, employment or participation in University sponsored extra-curricular activities." A guide explaining the speech code listed examples of prohibited conduct, including:

> *You exclude someone from a study group because that person is of a different race, sex, or ethnic origin that you are. . . . You display a confederate flag on the door of your room in your residence hall . . . You comment in a derogatory way about a particular person or group's physical appearance or sexual orientation, or their cultural origins, or religious beliefs.*

Many complaints were filed against students under this and other similar speech codes. At the University of Michigan, a biopsychology graduate student challenged the policy, arguing that discussion of certain controversial theories in his field, which examines differences in personality traits and mental abilities, might violate the policy.

In 1989, a federal court agreed with him. In the decision *Doe v. University of Michigan,* the court struck down the school's speech code, explaining that the policy was both overbroad (prohibiting protected speech in order to suppress unprotected speech) and vague (not clearly informing a person what type of expression is allowed). In 1991, supporters of campus speech codes suffered another setback at the University of Wisconsin. In this case, *UWM Post v. Board of Regents of University of Wisconsin,* the school's newspaper led the charge against restrictions on free expression included in the university's speech code.

"... the suppression of speech, even where the speech's content appears to have little value and great costs, amounts to governmental thought control."

—*U.S. District Court ruling in* UWM Post v. Board of Regents of University of Wisconsin, *1991*

Despite these legal defeats, campus speech codes still exist at colleges and universities across the United States. In 1994, the U.S. Department of Education threatened to take away federal funding from universities if they tolerated an environment that violated civil rights laws against discrimination by race or sex. Since then most schools have protected the speech codes by narrowly defining them and including them in harassment or diversity policies.

Campus speech codes remain the focus of intense debate and legal battles. Supporters of the codes maintain that they are necessary to create an educational environment free of hostility and intimidation and that they send a clear message that any form of bigotry will not be tolerated. Opponents of these policies argue that the codes have had a chilling effect by placing political correctness (the avoidance of expression that can be perceived to exclude or insult people or groups) over their constitutional right to free expression. They often feel that this loss of liberty is made even worse because it occurs on college campuses, which they feel are places where all views are entitled to be heard, explored, supported, or rejected.

HATE CRIMES

Cities and states soon joined colleges and universities in creating policies prohibiting certain hateful forms of expression. In 1990, St. Paul, Minnesota, adopted a "bias-motivated crime ordinance" that made it a crime to display a symbol that "arouses anger, alarm or resentment in others on the basis of race, color, creed, religion, or gender."

This law was challenged in the 1992 U.S. Supreme Court case *R.A.V. v. City of St. Paul, Minnesota.* This case centered on the actions of a white juvenile who burned a cross on the yard of a neighboring black family. His conviction under the St. Paul's antibias law was unanimously overturned by the Court, which found that the law unconstitutionally prohibited a form of protected speech. In his decision, Justice Antonin Scalia noted that the offender could have been charged under many other laws that had been violated. He explained, "Let there be no mistake about our belief that burning a cross in someone's front yard is reprehensible. But St. Paul has sufficient means at its disposal to prevent such behavior without adding the First Amendment to the fire."

But a year after the *R.A.V.* decision, the U.S. Supreme Court unanimously upheld a law that gave stiffer sentences for racially motivated assaults than for other types of assaults. In *Wisconsin v. Mitchell,* the Court reasoned that Wisconsin's Statute on Hate Crimes, passed in 1989, did not violate the First Amendment's guarantee of free expression because it was aimed at conduct, in this case an attack by a black youth on a white victim because of his race, and not speech.

Since the Wisconsin hate crime law was upheld, many other states have followed with similar laws that increase the penalty for crimes if it can be proven that they were committed because of bigotry. Opponents believe that the Constitution prohibits increasing the punishment for a crime based on the thoughts, feelings, or expression that provoked it. Supporters of these laws argue that a crime motivated by hatred of a particular group is worse than a crime motivated only by hatred of an individual because hate crimes are more likely to lead to widespread retaliation, emotional harm, and unrest in a community.

Russell Jones and his wife Laura, victims of a racially motivated crime at the center of *R.A.V. v. City of St. Paul, Minnesota,* pose in front of the Supreme Court in Washington, D.C., in 1991. *(Robert Sherbow/Getty Images)*

THE FIGHT OVER FLAG BURNING

Few expressions of symbolic speech spur more anger than the act of desecrating an American flag. During and after the Vietnam War era, some protesters of the war burned the American flag as a powerful expression of their political views. To many others, burning a flag was simply an unacceptably disrespectful rejection of a treasured national symbol.

An important flag desecration incident took place on a sunny summer day in Dallas, Texas, in 1984. Gregory Johnson, joined by about 100 demonstrators protesting President Ronald Reagan's policies, unfurled an American flag, doused it in kerosene, and set

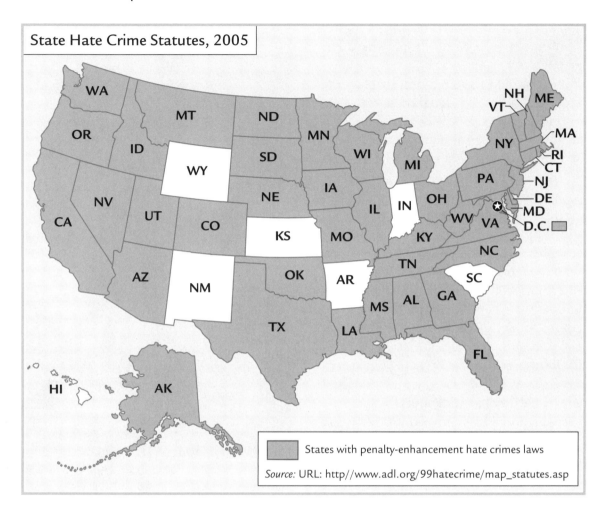

State Hate Crime Statutes, 2005

States with penalty-enhancement hate crimes laws

Source: URL: http//www.adl.org/99hatecrime/map_statutes.asp

it on fire. As the flag burned, the group chanted, "America, the red, white, and blue, we spit on you!"

Johnson was arrested under a Texas law prohibiting desecration of the American flag. He was soon convicted, fined $2,000, and sentenced to a year in prison. Johnson fought his conviction, which was overturned by the Texas Court of Appeals. The state then appealed the case to the U.S. Supreme Court.

In 1989, almost five years after Johnson burned the American flag, the Supreme Court upheld the lower court's ruling in *Texas v. Johnson.* The justices were bitterly divided in this case over whether a person can be prosecuted for flag desecration because of First Amendment protections of free speech. In the majority opinion,

A BRIEF HISTORY OF THE PROTECTION OF THE STARS AND STRIPES

Feelings among Americans about protecting the flag from abuse were not always as intense as they were in the late 20th century. For more than 100 years in U.S. history, there were no federal laws protecting the flag, and until the Civil War, little attention was paid to its patriotic value. After the Civil War, there was a movement to protect the flag from those who used it for advertising or political campaign purposes, but companies and politicians continued to use the flag successfully for their purposes.

In the late 19th century, concern over immigration and labor unrest led many to feel that American values were threatened, and increasingly the flag came to be seen as a symbol of those values. By 1932, all states had passed laws banning the desecration of the flag, though cases of deliberate flag burning were almost nonexistent until the 1960s.

Gregory Johnson, the defendant in the Supreme Court case *Texas v. Johnson,* speaks against a proposed constitutional amendment banning flag desecration outside the U.S. Capitol in 1990. *(Cynthia Johnson/ Getty Images)*

"If we seek to punish those who express views we don't share, then we—not the flag burners—begin to erode the . . . freedoms that make America the greatest democracy the world has ever known."

—*Senator Chuck Robb, 2000*

Justice William Brennan wrote, "We do not consecrate the flag by punishing its desecration, for in doing so we dilute the freedom that this cherished emblem represents." Justice William Rehnquist disagreed, arguing in his dissenting opinion that the flag was deserving of special protection because it was "unique" and "millions and millions of Americans regard it with an almost mystical reverence . . . deep awe and respect."

The uproar did not end with the *Johnson* decision allowing the burning of the American flag as a protected form of free speech under the First Amendment. In 1989, President George H. W. Bush endorsed a constitutional amendment to overturn the *Johnson* ruling and prohibit certain forms of flag desecration. This proposal and others that followed have been defeated in Congress by small margins.

The conflicts over the First Amendment's rights to free speech and a free press seen in the last decades of the 20th century challenged and ultimately extended the rights to free expression guaranteed by the Constitution. Although these issues will almost certainly continue to be hotly debated, the legacy of this period is that government is allowed to punish illegal actions, not hateful beliefs.

8

The Present and Future of Free Speech and Press

As the United States approached the 21st century, the rights to free speech and press guaranteed by the First Amendment more than 200 years earlier continued to endure. But, as always, there were challenges. Among the leading questions facing the rights to free speech and free press were old conflicts over decency and national security and new arguments over how to manage the massive expansion in information technology, particularly the Internet.

> "When I took office only high energy physicists had ever heard of what is called the World Wide Web . . . Now even my cat has his own Web site."
>
> —*President Bill Clinton, 1996*

THE INTERNET

The explosive growth in popularity of the Internet during the 1990s presented many of the same free speech and free press conflicts that the introduction of the printing press, radio, film, and television did decades and centuries earlier. With technology moving faster than the law's ability to keep up with it, many worried about what effect cyberspace would have on its users, particularly children.

These concerns led to the Communications Decency Act (CDA) of 1996. This law created content regulations on the Internet similar to those on television, including measures prohibiting the transmission of indecent material to children. Within 15 minutes of its passage, the CDA was challenged by a lawsuit on the grounds that it ignored First Amendment protections to free speech and free press.

Supporters of the CDA in Congress and President Bill Clinton, who signed the bill, quickly realized that censoring cyberspace was full of unique difficulties. Unlike newspapers, radio, and television, almost anyone with a computer and the know-how could publish their ideas on the Internet at very little cost. Opponents of the law

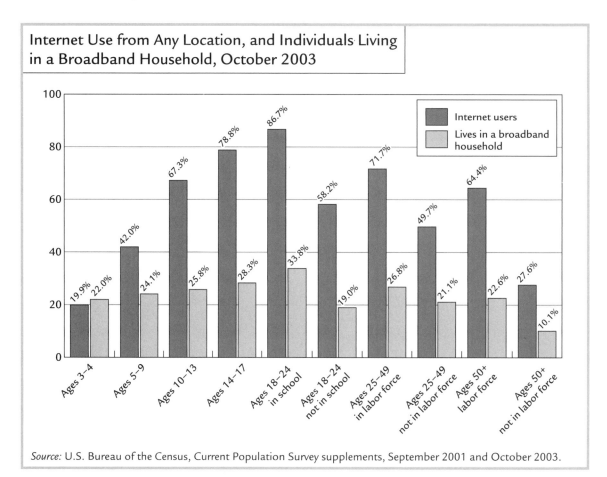

Internet Use from Any Location, and Individuals Living in a Broadband Household, October 2003

Source: U.S. Bureau of the Census, Current Population Survey supplements, September 2001 and October 2003.

The growth of Internet users and increased availability of broadband connections has raised free speech concerns.

argued that it was impractical and unfair in the way that it attempted to limit forms of protected speech in order to punish forms of speech (such as indecent images of children) against which laws already existed.

The U.S. Supreme Court agreed with the CDA's opponents and unanimously overturned the law in the 1997 case of *Reno v. American Civil Liberties Union.* Explaining that the CDA would unconstitutionally restrict expression on the Internet, the Court noted, "It is true that we have repeatedly recognized the governmental interest in protecting children from harmful materials . . . But that interest does not justify an unnecessarily broad suppression of speech addressed to adults. As we have explained, the government may not reduce the adult population . . . to . . . only what is fit for children."

The Court backed up its reasoning by illustrating how, under the CDA, a parent sending her 17-year-old child in college an e-mail including information about birth control could be sent to jail under certain circumstances, comparing the overbroad though well-intentioned law to "burning a house to cook a dinner."

Although the CDA failed, efforts to ensure that the Internet does not endanger youth continue. Since the late 1990s, software that filters out material possibly considered offensive (sometimes called content filtering software or "censorware") has become more sophisticated, popular, and effective. In light of the Supreme Court's clear protection of First Amendment rights to free speech and press as applied to the Internet, these types of options will likely become even more attractive to those who wish to limit the content brought into their homes via the Internet.

> "We are creating a world where anyone, anywhere may express his or her beliefs, no matter how singular, without fear of being coerced into silence or conformity."
>
> —*John Perry Barlow,*
> A Declaration of the
> Independence of
> Cyberspace, *1996*

THE DEBATE OVER MUSIC CENSORSHIP AND TELEVISION STANDARDS

The end of the 20th century and the beginning of the 21st century also brought intense battles over indecency in radio and television. In the 1980s, many religious and parents' groups mounted campaigns to limit the lyrical content of recording artists. The most prominent of these groups was the Parents Music Resource Center (PMRC), which called for labeling of recordings whose themes or imagery related to sexuality, violence, drug or alcohol use, suicide, or cults. Following years of pressure from the PMRC and a series of hearings in the U.S. Senate, the Recording Industry Association of America agreed in 1990 to adopt a labeling system for some music that was popular with youths.

Although these warning labels have been common since that time, neither side in the free expression in music debate is very happy. Supporters of voluntary labeling often argue that the labels do not go far enough in warning parents of a song's content and that punishments against stores that sell labeled music to minors should be stronger. They are also concerned that simply placing a label on the music actually makes it more attractive to the potential young consumer. Opponents of the labeling system contend that the restrictions are unfairly applied and lead some music retailers to censor labeled music out of fear that protest and bad publicity may lead to consumer boycotts.

Since the 1990s, a compromise has taken place. The labels still exist, though attempts to expand their scope and efforts to pass more restrictive legislation have failed. Many recording artists now release two versions of their music, one with explicit lyrics and the other with an edited, "cleaner" version, allowing both sides of the debate comfort that their concerns are being addressed.

Voluntary guidelines brought about following pressure from groups concerned about the effects of indecency on children have also been implemented in television. In the mid-1990s, the major national television networks adopted a rating system similar to the movie rating system that has existed for decades. The ratings, TC-Y (suitable for all children), TV-7 (acceptable for kids seven and under), and TV-MA (appropriate for mature viewers only) were designed to provide parents with clear expectations of a show's content. The ratings were also to be integrated with a technological innovation called the V-Chip (V-stands for violence), which is capable of blocking the transmission of a show based on its rating. This small electronic device was required by Congress to be installed in all new televisions by the year 2000.

THE RISE AND FALL OF THE V-CHIP

Although the V-Chip was introduced as a revolutionary tool that would allow parents to effectively filter what their children see and hear, the American public has largely ignored it. This belief is supported by a 2003 survey that studied households given active V-Chip technical support. One hundred and ten families with children were given new TV sets containing V-Chips, and most of the parents received detailed operating instructions. At the end of one year, 77 families reported that they had never tried the device, while just 8 percent claimed to be using it. This percentage is likely to be higher than that for usage among the general population, who have never received any training. Many jokingly explain that moms and dads will be unable to use any filtering device that requires programming skills without persuading their 11-year-old to show them how.

However, most research has shown that very few Americans use the TV ratings as a guideline for viewing and even fewer rely on the V-Chip, though "child locks" on the increasingly popular cable and satellite television services have proven attractive to parents. These methods of restricting what is seen and heard are acceptable to most First Amendment advocates, who are primarily concerned with how government, not private businesses, restricts free expression.

In 2004, a furor over what kind of expression may be shown on television erupted during the halftime show of the Super Bowl. During a performance, singer Justin Timberlake tore at the shirt of singing partner Janet Jackson, briefly revealing her near-naked breast. Few viewers believed Timberlake's claim that the incident was a "wardrobe malfunction," and millions were outraged over the stunt, broadcast during what is traditionally the most widely viewed program of the year among adults and children.

The outrage quickly ignited a discussion over not only what should be shown on television but also what is said in various forms of media. Particular attention was given to morning radio program personalities known as "shock jocks" because of their often-controversial content. Within weeks, the Federal Communications Commission (FCC) issued some of the largest fines for indecency in its history against companies that owned popular morning radio programs. The FCC then called for a 1000 percent increase in the maximum fine amount allowed for each incident of indecency over the airwaves ($27,500 to $275,000).

How this issue and the wider topic of indecency on radio and television will be resolved is unclear. The

This 2004 cartoon by John Cole comments on the growing crackdown by the Federal Communications Commission (FCC) on broadcast material considered indecent. (*John Cole,* The Herald Sun, *Durham, NC*)

battle lines between those who want to be protected from what they consider indecent material and those who argue that those offended should just not watch or listen are sharply drawn. The U.S. Supreme Court may ultimately determine the course of this issue, as it has in so many other past controversies over freedom of speech and the press.

SEPTEMBER 11 AND ITS IMPACT ON FREE EXPRESSION

Another historically complicated issue of freedom of speech and the press was tragically revisited on September 11, 2001, when the World Trade Center, in New York City, and the Pentagon, outside Washington, D.C., were attacked by Islamic fundamentalist terrorists who had hijacked and intentionally crashed airplanes into these crowded and symbolically important buildings (another hijacked plane, believed to be targeted for the U.S. Capitol, crashed in a Pennsylvania field after passengers struggled with terrorists). Almost 3,000 people were killed in these attacks.

As the United States began to emerge from the horrible shock of these terrorist strikes, Americans immediately sought to find ways to prevent such attacks from happening again. Many believed that the United States was vulnerable to these attacks partially because it is such an open society, with a high tolerance for dissenting political voices. A few months after September 11, Congress overwhelmingly passed a law entitled the USA PATRIOT Act (Uniting and Strengthening America by Providing Appropriate Tools Required to Intercept and Obstruct Terrorism), intended to more closely and effectively monitor those who might plot against the nation. The USA PATRIOT Act also included measures to shield information from the press and others in order to preserve national security.

Initially, these restrictions on the First Amendment's rights to dissent and to know were widely tolerated by an American public still shaken by the terrorist attacks. However, opinions soon shifted as the United States became involved militarily in antiterrorism battles in Afghanistan and Iraq. The war in Iraq particularly sparked the debate over free speech and free press during wartime.

Opponents of the war and what they believed were the USA PATRIOT Act's unfair restrictions on the First Amendment pleaded their case. These protesters were often labeled disloyal and unpatriotic. Responding to complaints that President George W. Bush's policies were chipping away at First Amendment protections to free speech and free press, U.S. Attorney General John Ashcroft said, "To those who scare peace-loving people with phantoms of lost liberty, my message is this: Your tactics only aid terrorists, for they erode our national unity and diminish our resolve."

The war on terrorism noticeably affected freedom of the press. Parts of the Freedom of Information Act were revoked. Measures were approved vastly increasing the number of documents that could be marked as "classified," limiting their access by the press and the public. To those who supported these measures, such steps were necessary to protect the nation; to those who opposed them, these restrictions violated the First Amendment and prevented important information from being shared with the American public.

> "To announce that there must be no criticism of the president or that we are to stand by the president right or wrong is not only unpatriotic . . . it is morally treasonable to the American public."
>
> —*President Theodore Roosevelt, 1902*

"TURNING THE LIGHT ON OURSELVES"
The *New York Times* and Iraq War Reporting

Criticism of the role of the press during wartime came from an unusual source during the Iraq War: the press itself. In May 2004, the *New York Times* published an editorial admitting that the newspaper had fallen far short of its standards in its reporting on the events leading to the U.S. invasion of Iraq. In an unusually apologetic tone, the *Times* explained that it had relied too heavily on the claims of sources within Iraq who had provided information to the press and the U.S. government, noting, ". . . we have found a number of instances of coverage that was not as rigorous [strict and accurate] as it should have been. . . . Looking back, we wish we had been more aggressive in re-examining the claims as new evidence emerged—or failed to emerge." Supporters of the *New York Times* praised the newspaper's honest self-analysis and explained that it would improve press accuracy in the future. Critics countered that the *Times* did not offer any solutions to ensure that such mistakes would not happen again and that the newspaper's careless coverage gave support to those who believed in the old adage that "the first casualty of war is truth."

Media coverage of the war saw an extension of the pool reporting system that had been popular during the Gulf War of the early 1990s, in which reporters shared stories and images with other news outlets. During the fighting in Iraq, embedded reporters, known as "embeds," traveled with U.S. military units and were represented on all major television networks and many leading newspapers. Critics argued that because embeds were essentially part of an American fighting force, they would be easily manipulated and might fail to report accurately. Others believed that because the embeds traveled with U.S. military they were able to bring clear and critically important firsthand reports from the front.

Advancements in technology's ability to transmit information more quickly and globally will likely make restrictions of the press more difficult in the United States and around the world. How Americans in the 21st century and beyond will view dissent during time of war will likely be determined by how much they trust their news sources and their government and by how severely they view the threat to their security.

THE FUTURE OF FREE SPEECH AND PRESS

Perhaps the most important factor determining the future of the First Amendment freedoms of speech and the press will be how well these rights and responsibilities are taught and learned in American schools. Elementary, middle, and high school students in the United States do not have all of the same rights as adults (18 years and older). But they do enjoy most free speech and even free press rights, though student free speech rights can be curtailed if they are determined to significantly disrupt classes and other school activities.

The teaching of civics courses in U.S. schools has dwindled over the past few decades. As a result, many are concerned that generations of American students miss out on essential knowledge that strengthens democracy and society: that the United States is a nation born out of dissent and has expanded previously unknown rights to its citizens through open and often hard-fought debate. This ignorance would likely worry countless

STUDENTS' RIGHTS TO FREEDOM OF PRESS
The *Hazelwood* Case

One effective way that young people can learn about freedom of the press is by joining the staff of their school's newspaper. But do student journalists have the same First Amendment rights as professional journalists? That question was the focus of a controversy in 1983 at East Hazelwood High School in Missouri, when the school's principal removed two pages containing articles about pregnant teenagers and divorce, which he considered inappropriate and possibly disruptive for students.

The student writers sued, claiming that their First Amendment rights to freedom of press were violated. In 1988, the U.S. Supreme Court took the case. In *Hazelwood v. Kuhlmeier,* the Court struck down the decision of the appeals court, which had ruled that the students' First Amendment rights were violated. The Supreme Court explained that the newspaper was not a public forum and "educators do not offend the First Amendment by exercising editorial control over the style and content of student speech in school-sponsored expressive activities so long as their actions are reasonably related to legitimate pedagogical [teaching] concerns."

Americans of the past, from the founders to civil rights workers, that a nation whose citizens do not know and appreciate its valuable rights will be too willing to give them up.

In 1962, President John F. Kennedy expressed his support for free speech and free press in U.S. society, saying "A nation that is afraid to let its people judge the truth and falsehood of ideas in an open market is a nation that is afraid of its people." The future of the First Amendment's rights to free expression will depend on how much faith the American people have in this belief. The clearest theme learned from the history of the American rights of free speech and free press is that they often lead to complex and uncomfortable dissent and debate, but ultimately serve as the best guarantees

Cartoonist Henry Payne suggests that true American patriotism was founded on confidence in the power of free expression. *(Henry Payne, reprinted by permission of United Feature Syndicate, Inc.)*

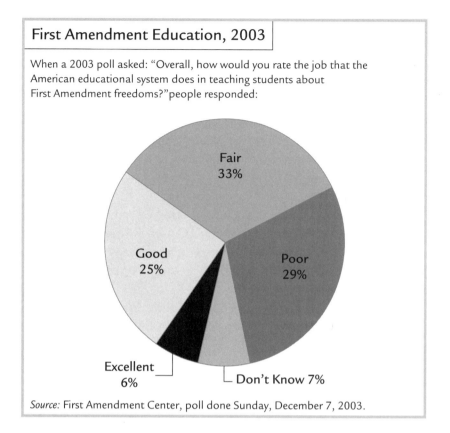

First Amendment Education, 2003

When a 2003 poll asked: "Overall, how would you rate the job that the American educational system does in teaching students about First Amendment freedoms?"people responded:

Fair 33%

Poor 29%

Good 25%

Excellent 6%

Don't Know 7%

Source: First Amendment Center, poll done Sunday, December 7, 2003.

that society will honor the qualities most valued by the framers of the First Amendment—knowledge, tolerance, and liberty—that cherish not only the strength of the United States but also the rights of all American citizens.

Glossary

abolitionist   A person who supported the elimination of slavery from the United States.

American Civil Liberties Union (ACLU)   The oldest and most prominent First Amendment advocacy organization in the United States.

anarchist   A person who believes that all forms of government should be abolished.

blacklist   A list of people out of favor because of their known or suspected beliefs.

censorship   The suppression or restriction of written or spoken material that is considered offensive.

"clear and present danger" test   Guidelines established by the U.S. Supreme Court in the 1919 case *Schenck v. United States* explaining that written or spoken expression can be restricted if it is likely to cause significant evils.

Communications Decency Act (CDA)   The first federal law designed to place content restrictions on Internet content; it was later struck down by the U.S. Supreme Court.

Comstockery   The early 20th-century efforts designed to protect public morals, named for postal official Anthony Comstock, which were criticized by detractors as unconstitutional restrictions on free expression.

"dangerous tendency" test   Guidelines articulated by the U.S. Supreme Court in the 1919 case *Abrams v. United States* that allowed restriction of the words of a speaker or writer if they led to an action that could endanger public peace or national security.

Deep Throat   The anonymous source who provided information to reporters Bob Woodward and Carl Bernstein during the Watergate scandal (voluntarily revealed in 2005 as former high-ranking FBI official W. Mark Felt).

embedded   Term used to describe reporters who travel as part of a U.S. military unit during the Iraq War.

fighting words   Terms or phrases considered so libelous and insulting that they will likely lead to a violent response.

Federal Communications Commission (FCC)   U.S. government agency that regulates communications by radio, television, wire, satellite, and cable.

Freedom of Information Act (FOIA)   Federal law allowing access to most government agency records.

gag laws   Regulations that prohibit the expression of written or spoken words because of the effect they may have.

hate speech   Expression intended to hurt and intimidate someone because of his or her race, ethnicity, national origin, religion, sexual orientation, or disability.

heckler's veto   The suppression of speech because of the possibility of a violent reaction by opponents.

libel   Written words that are false, malicious, and often damaging to the reputation of another person.

licensing   The practice of requiring government approval for the publication of written material, popular in Great Britain before the 20th century.

malice   The intent to cause pain or distress without legal justification or excuse.

McCarthyism   Smearing opponents through unsupported accusations of disloyalty; it was named after the early 1950s senator, Joseph McCarthy.

muckrakers   Influential early 20th-century U.S. writers who exposed social, political, and economic problems in America's increasingly industrial society.

obscenity   Expression that may be considered offensive to morals, good taste, and accepted community standards.

Palmer Raids   The forced entries into homes, offices, and property of suspected political radical leaders by U.S. government officials; it was named for U.S. Attorney General A. Mitchell Palmer, who, during his time in office, led these raids.

Parents Music Resource Center (PMRC)   An organization formed in the 1980s to fight indecency in music that is popular with young people.

Pentagon Papers   The popular name given to the U.S. Department of Defense's secret documents detailing U.S. involvement in Vietnam. They were eventually published in the *New York Times*.

political correctness   Avoidance of expression that can be perceived to exclude or insult people or groups.

prior restraint   The prohibition of expression before it is spoken or published.

prurient interest   A morbid, degrading, and unhealthy interest in sexual material.

Red Scare   Specifically, the period from 1919 to the early 1920s during which fear of communist influence surged in the United States. May be applied to other similar occurrences in history.

safe harbor   The hours between 10:00 P.M. and 6:00 A.M. during which obscenity standards are relaxed because children are unlikely to be in the audience.

satire   A form of expression that seeks to amusingly ridicule individuals, societies, or institutions.

slander   Spoken words that are false, malicious, and often damaging to the reputation of another person.

speech codes   Policies particularly popular on college campuses designed to prohibit words or phrases that offend a person or group based on race, gender, ethnicity, religion, or sexual orientation.

Star Chamber   The secretive late 16th- and early 17th-century group of advisers to the British king that often prosecuted people who wrote or spoke critically of the king.

symbolic speech   The expression of beliefs through the use of silent action, such as wearing an armband, rather than words.

treason   The betrayal of one's own country through disloyalty or attempts to overthrow the government.

USA PATRIOT Act   Common name for the Uniting and Strengthening America by Providing Appropriate Tools Required to Intercept and Obstruct Terrorism Act, which included increased restrictions on press and public access to information.

V-Chip Device designed to allow parental control over television content.

Watergate An early 1970s political scandal involving crimes and coverups committed by or in the name of President Richard Nixon that was exposed by journalists and led to Nixon's resignation.

Wobblies Members of an early 20th-century labor union, the International Workers of the World, who were often at the center of controversy over free expression.

yellow journalism Description of reporting popular in the late 19th century, marked by intense competition between newspapers, an emphasis on scandalous stories, and often irresponsible treatment of stories.

Chronology

509–27 B.C.

- During the era of the Ancient Roman Empire, people are often jailed, exiled, or killed for spoken criticism of the government.

399 B.C.

- The Greek philosopher Socrates is tried and executed for his spoken criticism of Athenian society.

1215 A.D.

- The Magna Carta (Latin for "Great Charter") is signed in England, guaranteeing certain rights for noblemen.

1459

- Johann Gutenberg invents the movable type printing press in Germany.

1644

- English poet John Milton delivers a speech entitled *Areopagitica* in which he argues against official efforts to prohibit free speech and press.

1690

- The first British colonial newspaper in the Americas, *Publick Occurrences Both Foreign and Domestic,* is printed in Boston; the paper is shut down after only one issue because government leaders disapprove of its content.

1765

+ The British Parliament passes the Stamp Act, requiring publishers in the American colonies to pay a special tax to produce printed material.

1775

+ *March 23:* Virginia lawyer Patrick Henry famously proclaims, "Give me liberty or give me death!" during a meeting of the Continental Congress.
+ *April 19:* The Revolutionary War begins with the battles of Lexington and Concord.

1776

+ *January 10:* Thomas Paine publishes the pro-independence pamphlet *Common Sense,* which quickly becomes enormously popular and influential in the American colonies.
+ *June 12:* The Virginia Declaration of Rights is signed, specifically noting the importance of the freedom of the press.
+ *July 4:* The Declaration of Independence is signed in Philadelphia, giving birth to the United States of America.

1791

+ *December 15:* The Bill of Rights is approved, including the First Amendment, which guarantees the freedoms of speech and the press.

1798

+ The Alien and Sedition acts are passed by Congress, expanding the government's power to punish "treasonable" activities.

1801

+ The Alien and Sedition acts expire.

1804

+ The New York case *People v. Croswell* helps lead states to enact laws allowing truth as a defense against charges of libel.

1829

+ David Walker publishes the abolitionist pamphlet *Appeal,* urging slaveholders to repent for their sins and trying to inspire active uprising by slaves.

1830s

♦ The number of newspapers in the United States grows to 1,200 from about 200 in 1800.

1831

♦ *January 1:* William Lloyd Garrison publishes the first issue of the influential abolitionist newspaper *The Liberator.*

1836

♦ *July 2:* Congress passes the Post Office Act, allowing states to refuse to deliver certain mail, including abolitionist publications.

1837

♦ *November 7:* Illinois publisher Elijah Lovejoy is murdered by an antiabolitionist mob.

1850s–60s

♦ Frederick Douglass becomes a leading abolitionist speaker and writer.

1863

♦ Stress on free speech and freedom of the press caused by the Civil War (1861–65) reaches its peak with the arrest of E. M. Fuller, editor of the *Newark* (New Jersey) *Evening Journal* and the shutting down of the *Chicago Times.*

1868

♦ The Fourteenth Amendment to the Constitution is ratified. Among its implied provisions it prohibits states from denying free expression rights.

1886

♦ A bomb explodes at Chicago's Haymarket Square following a protest by striking workers, anarchists who supported their cause, and replacement workers.

1890s

♦ Intense competition between newspapers leads to an emphasis on scandalous stories and often irresponsible reporting known as yellow journalism.

1898

◆ The Spanish-American War is covered intensely by American newspapers, leading to increased readership and charges of misuse of journalism's influence.

1901

◆ *September 14:* President William McKinley is assassinated by a son of Polish immigrants, leading to a crackdown on the free expression of political and ethnic minorities.

1905–17

◆ The labor union the Industrial Workers of the World, also known as the Wobblies, gains prominence through often controversial speeches and writings.

1906–16

◆ A group of journalists known as muckrakers advocates social reform through the publication of widely read exposés of political, corporate, and labor corruption.

1915

◆ The height of "Comstockery," named for U.S. Post Office agent Anthony Comstock, features efforts, including legislation, designed to protect public morality from offensive speech and writings.

1917

◆ *June 15:* Congress passes the Espionage Act, prohibiting the writing of disloyal, profane, or abusive material about the United States during wartime.

1918

◆ *May 16:* Congress passes the Sedition Act, making it a crime to support any country at war with the United States, and the Trading with the Enemy Act, requiring certified translations of some foreign-language publications.

1919

◆ *March 3:* In *Schenck v. United States,* the U.S. Supreme Court establishes the "clear and present danger" test for free expression, upholding the conviction of a man accused of violating the Espionage Act.

* ***November 10:*** In *Abrams v. United States,* the U.S. Supreme Court establishes the "dangerous tendency" test for free expression, upholding the conviction of five men who were protesting U.S. policy in Russia.

1920

* ***January 2:*** The first of the Palmer Raids of the homes, offices, and property of suspected political radical leaders, named for U.S. Attorney General A. Mitchell Palmer, highlight the period of fear of communism known as the Red Scare.
* The leading First Amendment rights organization, the American Civil Liberties Union (ACLU), is formed.

1921

* The Espionage and Sedition acts are repealed as Americans become increasingly concerned about the power of the government to restrict free expression.

1927

* The U.S. Supreme Court rules in *Near v. Minnesota* that a gag law designed to place prior restraint on irresponsible use of freedom of the press should not be allowed.

1930

* The Hays Code establishes standards of "good taste" for the movie industry.

1934

* The Federal Communication Commission (FCC) is created.

1938

* An issue of *Time* magazine featuring an article on the birth of a baby is banned in many cities on claims of indecency.

1940

* The Smith Act is passed by Congress, making it a crime to teach or encourage "subversive" ideas.

1941–45

◆ The United States fights in World War II with little vocal or written dissent from Americans.

1942

◆ *March 9:* The U.S. Supreme Court upholds the conviction of a person charged with violating a "fighting words" law in *Chaplinsky v. New Hampshire.*

1950

◆ *February 9:* Senator Joseph McCarthy begins making accusations that Communists had infiltrated the U.S. government, leading to the fearful era of "McCarthyism."

1954

◆ *March 10:* CBS News reporter Edward Murrow broadcasts a rebuke of Senator McCarthy's methods on the program *See It Now.*
◆ *April 22:* The Army-McCarthy hearings are covered live on television, leading to the end of Senator McCarthy's influence.

1957

◆ *April 22:* The U.S. Supreme Court rules in *Roth v. United States* that obscenity is not protected by the First Amendment, but does not clearly define what obscenity is.

1963

◆ *August 28:* The March on Washington draws more than 200,000 Civil Rights movement supporters and features the famous "I Have a Dream" speech by Martin Luther King, Jr.

1964

◆ *January 6:* In *New York Times v. Sullivan,* the U.S. Supreme Court rules that public officials have to prove a libelous statement is published with malicious intent.

1968

◆ *February 27:* Influential CBS News anchor Walter Cronkite delivers commentary questioning the wisdom of continued U.S. involvement in the Vietnam War.

- *August:* Anti–Vietnam War protesters clash with police outside the Democratic National Convention in Chicago.

1969

- *February 24:* The U.S. Supreme Court rules in *Tinker v. Des Moines* that public school students have the right to symbolic speech protest as long as they do not interfere with schoolwork or the rights of other students.

1971

- *June 13:* The first in a series of secret documents detailing U.S. involvement in Vietnam, known as the Pentagon Papers, is published in the *New York Times.*
- *June 30:* In *New York Times v. United States,* the U.S. Supreme Court rules that the newspaper has a First Amendment–protected right to publish the Pentagon Papers.

1972–74

- The Watergate scandal, resulting in the resignation of President Richard Nixon, is uncovered largely through the efforts of investigative journalists.

1974

- *May:* The Freedom of Information Act (FOIA), originally passed in 1966, is expanded to allow the right of access to federal agency records or information.
- *June 24:* In *Jenkins v. Georgia,* the U.S. Supreme Court rules that juries do not have complete authority to decide what is "patently offensive."

1977

- *August 12:* The ACLU files suit on behalf of a neo-Nazi group prevented from holding a rally in Skokie, Illinois; the neo-Nazis' right to rally is later upheld.

1978

- *July 3:* The U.S. Supreme Court rules that the Federal Communication Commission has the right to fine broadcasters for indecent language in *FCC v. Pacifica.*

1985

♦ The Parents Music Resource Center (PMRC) is founded to denounce what it believes are obscene and violent themes in popular music and their effect on young people.

1988

♦ *January 13:* In *Hazelwood v. Kuhlmeier,* the U.S. Supreme Court expands the power of school administrators to limit the free press rights of student journalists.
♦ *February 24:* In *Hustler v. Falwell,* the Supreme Court rules that satire directed at public figures is a protected form of speech.

1989

♦ *June 21:* The U.S. Supreme Court rules in *Texas v. Johnson* that First Amendment rights of free speech prohibit the prosecution for flag desecration.
♦ *September 29:* In *Doe v. University of Michigan,* the U.S. Supreme Court strikes down the school's speech code on the grounds that it is overbroad and vague.

1990–91

♦ The Persian Gulf War brings increased restrictions on press coverage of military operations.

1991

♦ *October 11:* A federal court supports a campus newspaper's charges against a college speech code in *UWM Post v. Board of Regents of University of Wisconsin.*

1992

♦ *June 22:* In *R.A.V. v. City of St. Paul, Minnesota,* the Supreme Court overturns St. Paul's anti-bias-motivated crime law because it punishes forms of protected speech.

1993

♦ In *Wisconsin v. Mitchell,* the U.S. Supreme Court upholds Wisconsin's Statute on Hate Crimes because it focuses on conduct, leading other states to pass hate crime laws.

1996

+ *February 1:* The Communications Decency Act is passed by Congress, which includes regulation on Internet content.

1997

+ *June 26:* The U.S. Supreme Court strikes down the Communications Decency Act in *Reno v. ACLU* on the grounds that it violates First Amendment rights to free expression.

2001

+ *October 25:* In response to the terrorist attacks on the United States on September 11, 2001, Congress passes the USA PATRIOT Act, which increases restrictions on press and public access to information.

2003

+ *March 20:* The Iraq War begins, introducing the use of embedded reporters (embeds) who travel as part of U.S. military units.

2004

+ *February 1:* A musical performance featuring the near-naked breast of singer, Janet Jackson, is broadcasted during the halftime of the Super Bowl, sparking a crackdown on indecency by the FCC.
+ *summer:* "Free speech zones" are established outside the Democratic and Republican National Conventions in Boston and New York City, respectively, in an attempt to balance concerns over security and free expression.
+ *November 11:* More than 60 ABC television network affiliates canceled the Veterans Day broadcast of *Saving Private Ryan* because of fear of fines by the FCC for the swearing in the movie.

2005

+ *January:* A survey released by the Knight Foundation shows that more than one-third of U.S. high school students believe that the First Amendment goes "too far" in the rights it guarantees and that only half of them believe that newspapers should be allowed to publish freely without government approval of stories (compared to 80 percent of school teachers and administrators).

Appendix

❦

Excerpts from Documents Relating to Freedom of Speech and the Press

❦

Cato's Letters—#15—
Of Freedom of Speech (1721)

Between 1720 and 1723 John Trenchard and Thomas Gordon, writing under the pseudonym (fake name) Cato, wrote and published many essays about freedom. These essays were published as *Cato's Letters* and they became very popular and influential throughout the British colonies in the Americas. One of the most widely quoted of *Cato's Letters* is #15, which stresses the importance of freedom of speech to all other freedoms. This essay is often credited with providing important early support for First Amendment rights to free expression.

❦

Without freedom of thought, there can be no such thing as wisdom; and no such thing as publick liberty, without freedom of speech: Which is the right of every man, as far as by it he does not hurt and control the right of another; and this is the only check which it ought to suffer, the only bounds which it ought to know.

This sacred privilege is so essential to free government, that the security of property; and the freedom of speech, always go together; and in those wretched countries where a man can not call his tongue his own, he can scarce call any thing else his own. Whoever would overthrow the liberty of the nation, must begin by subduing the freedom of speech; a thing terrible to publick traitors. . . .

That men ought to speak well of their governors, is true, while their governors deserve to be well spoken of; but to do publick mischief, without hearing of it, is only the prerogative and felicity of tyranny: A free people will be showing that they are so, by their freedom of speech.

The administration of government is nothing else, but the attendance of the trustees of the people upon the interest and affairs of the people. And as it is the part and business of the people, for whose sake alone all publick matters are, or ought to be, transacted, to see whether they be well or ill transacted; so it is the interest, and ought to be the ambition, of all honest magistrates, to have their deeds openly examined, and publickly scanned: Only the wicked governors of men dread what is said of them. . . .

Freedom of speech is the great bulwark of liberty; they prosper and die together: And it is the terror of traitors and oppressors, and a barrier against them. It produces excellent writers, and encourages men of fine genius. . . .

All ministers, therefore, who were oppressors, or intended to be oppressors, have been loud in their complaints against freedom of speech, and the license of the press; and always restrained, or endeavoured to restrain, both. In consequence of this, they have brow-beaten writers, punished them violently, and against law, and burnt their works. By all which they showed how much truth alarmed them, and how much they were at enmity with truth. . . .

Freedom of speech, therefore, being of such infinite importance to the preservation of liberty, every one who loves liberty ought to encourage freedom of speech. Hence it is that I, living in a country of liberty, and under the best prince upon earth, shall take this very favourable opportunity of serving mankind, by warning them of the hideous mischiefs that they will suffer, if ever corrupt and wicked men shall hereafter get possession of any state, and the power of betraying their master: And, in order to do this, I will show them by what steps they will probably proceed to accomplish their traitorous ends. This may be the subject of my next.

Valerius Maximus tells us, that Lentulus Marcellinus, the Roman consul, having complained, in a popular assembly, of the overgrown power of Pompey; the whole people answered him with a shout of approbation: Upon which the consul told them, "Shout on, gentlemen, shout on, and use those bold signs of liberty while you may; for I do not know how long they will be allowed you."

God be thanked, we Englishmen have neither lost our liberties, nor are in danger of losing them. Let us always cherish this matchless blessing, almost peculiar to ourselves; that our posterity may, many ages hence, ascribe their freedom to our zeal. The defense of liberty is a noble, a heavenly office; which can only be performed where liberty is. . . .

Source: University of Arkansas. Available online.
URL: http://www.uark.edu/depts/comminfo/cambridge/cato15.html.

Alien and Sedition Acts (1798)

Less than a decade after the passage of the Bill of Rights, the Alien and Sedition Acts presented the First Amendment with a major obstacle to its power. These laws were a response to the threat of war with France, and they led to intense debate. The Sedition Act gave the government wide powers to put down "treasonable activities." Eventually 25 men were arrested under the Sedition Act, mostly editors of newspapers critical of the government. Ten of them were convicted, and their newspapers were forced to close.

☙

SECTION 1

Be it enacted by the Senate and House of Representatives of the United States of America, in Congress assembled, That if any persons shall unlawfully combine or conspire together, with intent to oppose any measure or measures of the government of the United States, which are or shall be directed by proper authority, or to impede the operation of any law of the United States, or to intimidate or prevent any person holding a place or office in or under the government of the United States, from undertaking, performing or executing his trust or duty, and if any person or persons, with intent as aforesaid, shall counsel, advise or attempt to procure any insurrection, riot, unlawful assembly, or combination, whether such conspiracy, threatening, counsel, advice, or attempt shall have the proposed effect or not, he or they shall be deemed guilty of a high misdemeanor, and on conviction, before any court of the United States having jurisdiction thereof, shall be punished by a fine not exceeding five thousand dollars, and by imprisonment during a term not less than six months nor exceeding five years; and further, at the discretion of the court may beholden to find sureties for his good behaviour in such sum, and for such time, as the said court may direct.

SECTION 2

And be it farther enacted, That if any person shall write, print, utter or publish, or shall cause or procure to be written, printed, uttered or published, or shall knowingly and willingly assist or aid in writing, printing, uttering or publishing any false, scandalous and malicious writing or writings against the government of the United States, or either house of the Congress of the United States, or the President of the United States, with intent to defame the said government, or either house of the said Congress, or the said President, or to bring them, or either of them, into contempt or disrepute; or to excite against them, or either or any of them, the hatred of the good people of the United States, or to stir up sedition within the United States, or to excite any unlawful combinations therein, for opposing or resisting any law of the United States, or any act of the President of the United States, done in pursuance of any such law, or of the powers in him vested by the constitution of the United States, or to resist, oppose, or defeat any such law or act, or to aid, encourage or abet any hostile designs of any foreign nation against United States, their people or government, then such person, being thereof convicted before any court of the United States having jurisdiction thereof, shall be punished by a fine not exceeding two thousand dollars, and by imprisonment not exceeding two years.

SECTION 3

And be it further enacted and declared, That if any person shall be prosecuted under this act, for the writing or publishing any libel aforesaid, it shall be lawful for the defendant, upon the trial of the cause, to give in evidence in his defense, the truth of the matter contained in Republication charged as a libel. And the jury who shall try the cause, shall have a right to determine the law and the fact, under the direction of the court, as in other cases.

❧

SECTION 4

And be it further enacted, That this act shall continue and be in force until the third day of March, one thousand eight hundred and one, and no longer: Provided, that the expiration of the act shall not prevent or defeat a prosecution and punishment of any offence against the law, during the time it shall be in force.

APPROVED, July 14, 1798.

Source: The Avalon Project at Yale University. Available online. URL: http://www.yale.edu/lawweb/avalon/statutes/sedact.htm.

Inaugural Editorial of *The Liberator,* by William Lloyd Garrison (1831)

The struggle to end slavery in the United States gained critical public strength from the power of freedom of the press. Among the leading and earliest abolitionist writers was William Lloyd Garrison. The first issue of his antislavery paper, *The Liberator,* signified the beginning of journalism's influence in helping spread ideas that played a key role in motivating the movement that would eventually end slavery.

❧

During my recent tour for the purpose of exciting the minds of the people by a series of discourses on the subject of slavery, every place that I visited gave fresh evidence of the fact, that a greater revolution in public sentiment was to be effected in the free States—and particularly in New-England—than at the South. I found contempt more bitter, opposition more active, detraction more relentless, prejudice more stubborn, and apathy more frozen, than among slave-owners themselves. Of course, there were individual exceptions to the contrary. This state of things afflicted, but did not dishearten me. I determined, at every hazard, to lift up the standard of emancipation in the eyes of the nation, within sight of Bunker Hill and in the birthplace of liberty. That standard is now unfurled; and long may it float, unhurt by the spoliations of time or the missiles of a desperate foe—yea, till every chain be broken, and every bondman set free! Let Southern oppressors tremble—let their secret abettors tremble—let their Northern apologists tremble—let all the enemies of the persecuted black tremble . . .

I am aware that many object to the severity of my language; but is there not cause for severity? I will be as harsh as truth, and as uncompromising as justice. On this subject, I do not wish to think, or to speak, or write, with moderation. No! no! Tell a man whose house is on fire to give a moderate alarm; tell him to moderately rescue his wife from the hands of the ravisher; tell the mother to gradually extricate her babe from the fire into which it has fallen;—but urge me not to use moderation in a cause like the present. I am in earnest—I will not equivocate—I will not excuse—I will not retreat a single inch—AND I WILL BE HEARD. The apathy of the people is enough to make every statue leap from its pedestal, and to hasten the resurrection of the dead.

It is pretended, that I am retarding the cause of emancipation by the coarseness of my invective and the precipitancy of my measures. The charge is not true. On this question of my influence,—humble as it is,—is felt at this moment to a considerable extent, and shall be felt in coming years—not perniciously, but beneficially—not as a curse, but as a blessing; and posterity will bear testimony that I was right. I desire to thank God, that he enables me to disregard "the fear of man which bringeth a snare," and to speak his truth in its simplicity and power. . . .

Source: The University of the South. Available online.
URL: http://www.sewanee.edu/faculty/Willis/Civil_War/documents/Liberator.html.

Roth v. United States (1957)

Few, if any, First Amendment free speech issues have been as controversial as obscenity. The U.S. Supreme Court case *Roth v. United States* attempted to tackle this issue. The majority decision explained that obscenity was not constitutionally protected by First Amendment guarantees to free speech and press. The ruling also attempted to define what obscenity is (materials that are "utterly without redeeming social importance"), though interpretations and arguments over exactly what this definition means continue.

Justice Brennan delivered the opinion of the Court. . . .
The dispositive question is whether obscenity is utterance within the area of protected speech and press. Although this is the first time the

fear or apprehension of disturbance is not enough to overcome the right to freedom of expression. Any departure from absolute regimentation may cause trouble. Any variation from the majority's opinion may inspire fear. Any word spoken, in class, in the lunchroom, or on the campus, that deviates from the views of another person may start an argument or cause a disturbance. But our Constitution says we must take this risk, . . . and our history says that it is this sort of hazardous freedom—this kind of openness—that is the basis of our national strength and of the independence and vigor of Americans who grow up and live in this relatively permissive, often disputatious, society . . .

It is also relevant that the school authorities did not purport to prohibit the wearing of all symbols of political or controversial significance. . . . Clearly, the prohibition of expression of one particular opinion, at least without evidence that it is necessary to avoid material and substantial interference with schoolwork or discipline, is not constitutionally permissible. . . .

Under our Constitution, free speech is not a right that is given only to be so circumscribed that it exists in principle but not in fact. Freedom of expression would not truly exist if the right could be exercised only in an area that a benevolent government has provided as a safe haven for crackpots. The Constitution says that Congress (and the States) may not abridge the right to free speech. This provision means what it says. We properly read it to permit reasonable regulation of speech-connected activities in carefully restricted circumstances. But we do not confine the permissible exercise of First Amendment rights to a telephone booth or the four corners of a pamphlet, or to supervised and ordained discussion in a school classroom.

Source: Boston College. Available online.
URL: http://www.bc.edu/bc_org/aup/cas/comm/free-speech/tinker.html.

New York Times v. United States (1971)

The often combative relationship between the press and the military was the focus of the U.S. Supreme Court case *New York Times v. United States*. At issue was the publication by the *New York Times* of the Pentagon Papers, the Defense Department's secret documents describing the history of U.S. involvement in Vietnam. The unanimous court ruling was a smashing victory for those who supported expanded freedom of the press and a crushing defeat for those who claimed publication of these kinds of documents was dangerous to national security.

⸎

Justice Black, with whom Justice Douglas joins, concurring.

I adhere to the view that the Government's case against the *Washington Post* should have been dismissed and that the injunction against the *New York Times* should have been vacated without oral argument when the cases were first presented to this Court. I believe that every moment's continuance of the injunctions against these newspapers amounts to a flagrant, indefensible, and continuing violation of the First Amendment. Furthermore, after oral argument, I agree completely that we must affirm the judgment of the Court of Appeals for the District of Columbia Circuit and reverse the judgment of the Court of Appeals for the Second Circuit for the reasons stated by my Brothers Douglas and Brennan. In my view it is unfortunate that some of my Brethren are apparently willing to hold that the publication of news may sometimes be enjoined. Such a holding would make a shambles of the First Amendment.

Our Government was launched in 1789 with the adoption of the Constitution. The Bill of Rights, including the First Amendment, followed in 1791. Now, for the first time in the 182 years since the founding of the Republic, the federal courts are asked to hold that the First Amendment does not mean what it says, but rather means that the Government can halt the publication of current news of vital importance to the people of this country.

In seeking injunctions against these newspapers and in its presentation to the Court, the Executive Branch seems to have forgotten the essential purpose and history of the First Amendment. When the Constitution was adopted, many people strongly opposed it because the document contained no Bill of Rights to safeguard certain basic freedoms. They especially feared that the new powers granted to a central government might be interpreted to permit the government to curtail freedom of religion, press, assembly, and speech. In response to an overwhelming public clamor, James Madison offered a series of amendments to satisfy citizens that these great liberties would remain safe and beyond the power of government to abridge. Madison proposed what later became the First Amendment in three parts, two of which are set out below, and one of which proclaimed: "The people shall not be deprived or abridged of their right to speak, to write, or to publish their sentiments; and the freedom of the press, as one of the great bulwarks of liberty, shall be inviolable." . . . Madison and the other Framers of the First Amendment, able men that they were, wrote in language they earnestly believed could never be misunderstood: "Congress shall make no law . . . abridging the freedom . . . of the press. . . ." Both the history and language of the First Amendment support the view that the press must be left free to publish news, whatever the source, without censorship, injunctions, or prior restraints.

In the First Amendment the Founding Fathers gave the free press the protection it must have to fulfill its essential role in our democracy. The press was to serve the governed, not the governors. The Government's power to censor the press was abolished so that the press would remain forever free to censure the Government. The press was protected so that it could bare the secrets of government and inform the people. Only a free and unrestrained press can effectively expose deception in government. And paramount among the responsibilities of a free press is the duty to prevent any part of the government from deceiving the people and sending them off to distant lands to die of foreign fevers and foreign shot and shell. In my view, far from deserving condemnation for their courageous reporting, the *New York Times,* the *Washington Post,* and other newspapers should be commended for serving the purpose that the Founding Fathers saw so clearly. In revealing the workings of government that led to the Vietnam war, the newspapers nobly did precisely that which the Founders hoped and trusted they would do.

Source: Boston College. Available online.
URL: http://www.bc.edu/bc_org/aup/cas/comm/free-speech/nytvus.html.

U.S. Department of Defense Press Rules for Coverage of Iraq War (2003)

Responding to criticism that it did not allow journalists contact with fighting troops in 1991 during the Gulf War, the U.S. military devised new press rules allowing reporters to travel with combat units as long as they followed strict rules. About 500 reporters (one-fifth of them from foreign countries) were placed, or embedded, in military units. They could remain with units until the end of the war or until they decided to leave.

⁓

The media will be given access to operational combat missions, including mission preparation and debriefing, whenever possible. The media will be briefed as to what information may not be broadcast because of its sensitivity to military operations. For security reasons, commanders may impose news embargos and temporarily block communication transmissions.

1. The military cannot exclude reporters from combat areas to keep them safe. All reporters must sign an agreement waiving any legal action against the armed forces. Reporters are not allowed to carry firearms, use their own vehicles, or use lights at night (without permission).

2. Reporters can bring whatever communication equipment they want, but they must carry their own equipment. Reporters are encouraged to use lipstick and helmet-mounted cameras on combat missions.

3. The following information can be published or broadcast: approximate troop strength, approximate casualties, information and location of previous military targets and missions, names and hometowns of military units, service members' names and hometowns (with their permission).

4. The following cannot be published or broadcast because it could jeopardize operations and endanger lives: specific numbers of troops, aircraft, ships, and equipment; specific geographic location (unless released by the Department of Defense); information about future operations; rules of engagement (the circumstances under which a unit may fight).

5. Any violation of these rules will result in a reporter being sent away from the unit. These rules do not ban contact with reporters who are not embedded with the troops.

Source: Constitutional Rights Foundation. Available online. URL: http://crf-usa.org/Iraqwar_html/iraqwar_press.html.

Further Reading

Books

Alonso, Karen. Schenck v. United States: *Restrictions on Free Speech.* Berkeley Heights, N.J.: Enslow Publishers, 1999.

Day, Nancy. *Censorship, or Freedom of Expression?* Minneapolis: Lerner Publishing, 2000.

Egendorf, Laura K. *At Issue: Should There Be Limits to Free Speech?* Detroit: Greenhaven Press, 2003.

Fireside, Harvey. New York Times v. Sullivan: *Affirming Freedom of the Press.* Berkeley Heights, N.J.: Enslow Publishers, 1999.

Kennedy, Sheila Suess, ed. *Free Expression in America: A Documentary History.* Westport, Conn.: Greenwood Press, 1999.

King, David. *The Right to Speak Out.* Brookfield, Conn.: Millbrook Press, 1997.

Articles

"Too Much Freedom?" *The Atlantic Monthly,* April 2003, p. 37.

Trout, Paul. "Free Speech and the Academic Mission." *Phi Kappa Phi Forum,* fall 2001, p. 3.

Wilson, Mike. "Freedom of Speech: How Far Does it Go?" *Cobblestone,* January 1999, p. 2.

Web Sites

American Booksellers Foundation for Free Expression. "KidSpeak: Where Kids Speak Up for Free Speech." Available online. URL: http://www.kidspeakonline.org.

Detroit News. "Losing Liberty: A Detroit News Editorial Page Series."
    Available online. URL: http://www.detnews.com/specialreports/
    2003/liberty/index.htm.
First Amendment Center. "Hate Speech and Campus Speech Codes."
    Available online. URL: http://www.firstamendmentcenter.org/
    speech/pubcollege/topic.aspx?topic=campus_speech_codes.
Newseum: The Interactive Museum of News. "War Stories." Available
    online. URL: http://www.newseum.org/warstories/technology/
    flash.htm.
Salon.com. "Playing Games with Free Speech." Available online. URL:
    http://www.salon.com/tech/feature/2002/05/06/games_as_speech.

Bibliography

Curtis, Michael Kent. *Free Speech: The People's Darling Privilege.* Durham, N.C.: Duke University Press, 2000.

Eastland, Terry. *Freedom of Expression in the Supreme Court.* Lanham, Md.: Rowman and Littlefield, 2000.

Godwin, Mike. *CyberRights: Defending Free Speech in the Digital Age.* Cambridge, Mass.: MIT Press, 2003.

Goldstein, Robert Justin. *Flag Burning and Free Speech—The Case* of Texas v. Johnson. Lawrence: University Press of Kansas, 2000.

Greenwalt, Kent. *Fighting Words.* Princeton, N.J.: Princeton University Press, 1995.

Hentoff, Nat. *Free Speech for Me—But Not for Thee: How the American Left and Right Relentlessly Censor Each Other.* New York: HarperCollins, 1993.

Powe, Lucas. *The Fourth Estate and the Constitution: Freedom of the Press in America.* Berkeley: University of California Press, 1992.

Richards, Robert D. *Freedom's Voice: The Perilous Present and Uncertain Future of the First Amendment.* Farmington Hills, Mich.: G. K. Hall & Company, 2000.

Smith, Jeffrey Alan. *War and Press Freedom: The Problem of Prerogative Power.* New York: Oxford University Press, 1999.

Strum, Philippa. *When the Nazis Came to Skokie: Freedom for Speech We Hate.* Lawrence: University Press of Kansas, 1999.

Sunstein, Cass R. *Why Societies Need Dissent.* Cambridge, Mass.: Harvard University Press, 2003.

Index

Page numbers in *italic* indicate photographs. Page numbers in **boldface** indicate box features and margin quotations. Page numbers followed by *m* indicate maps. Page numbers followed by *t* indicate tables or graphs. Page numbers followed by *g* indicate glossary entries. Page numbers followed by *c* indicate chronology entries.